THEY GROW IN SILENCE
—the deaf child and his family

by Eugene D. Mindel, M.D.
Director, Child Psychiatry Services
Michael Reese Hospital

and

McCay Vernon, Ph.D.
Professor of Psychology
Western Maryland College

With a Foreword by
Roy R. Grinker, Sr., M.D.

Published by
National Association of the Deaf
Silver Spring, Maryland

To Sidney

he could talk to anyone

CONTENTS

Preface

In the spring of 1966, when the Project for the Deaf was in the planning stage at Michael Reese Hospital, Dr. Vernon and I met. Dr. Vernon, then at the University of Illinois, was hired as the planning director for the project; subsequently he became project director. I was completing two years active duty as a Naval Medical Officer. Our first meeting was to discuss my future role as child psychiatrist for the project, and to arrange sign language tutoring for my wife and myself.

I had already become acquainted with the deaf community while still in medical school. With two fellow junior medical students, I worked in the infirmary at Gallaudet College, Washington, D.C., the world's only college exclusively for the deaf. It cannot be said that it was a thoroughly sophisticating experience, for it was only after 1966 that I became aware of the full consequences of deafness. The experience at Gallaudet did serve, however, to help master the initial awkwardness that hearing people experience with deaf people, and I learned finger spelling and some sign language.

During the ensuing eight years, I never stopped thinking about that experience. I had a recurrent dream in which I met a deaf person and conversed using finger spelling.* A few times, there were actual attempts to use these limited skills, but real understanding or closeness with deaf persons was never achieved. The reasons for this failure have only become clear in the last three years, and form much of the thesis of this work.

While in psychiatric training, my thoughts about deaf people achieved greater definition. Since spoken language in human beings is so significant in establishing relationships, what could the effects be on mental development of not having a fully developed verbal language capacity? And beyond this, what changes take place in personality consequent to this lack?

* * * * * * * *

*I have since discovered that it is not uncommon for people who are attempting to learn a new language to have dreams in which they are conversing in the new language, rather than their native language. This was discovered during discussions of language development with first year residents in a child psychiatry seminar which I conducted at the Illinois State Psychiatric Institute, 1969-1970. The residents of that group came from diverse cultural backgrounds. Apparently, as the individual becomes more familiar and comfortable in using a new language — in this case, English — the dreams in which the individual is speaking English diminish in frequency or disappear altogether.

Such experiences suggest to the psychoanalyst or the psychoanalytically oriented psychiatrist the process of dream work operating to overcome difficult and anxiety producing circumstances inherent in adjustment to a new country and new language. A similar phenomenon was apparently operating in my case. The unfamiliar community and language in this case was manual communication and the deaf community. Since working more actively with deaf individuals and becoming more comfortable in the use of manual communication, I have not again had such dreams. Dream analysis beyond the level at which dream fragment is presented would, in each individual, reveal the deeper nature of the importance of communication to him.

But, time was short then and these questions could not be carried into an investigation.

The establishment of the Project for the Deaf in September, 1966, offered the opportunity for such an investigation. It brought together a group of people with somewhat diverse backgrounds but united by a common interest: to help deaf people through seeking a better understanding of their development and problems. Throughout the project, the distillate of many hours of discussions was always the same basic issues. Of these, perhaps the most fundamental is: *If communication difficulty strikes at the heart of the deaf person's plight, why do so many still advocate the use of a method of communication with so many inherent difficulties?* Beyond this, why do passions rise so high when these issues are discussed? For those who have come into work with deaf people without prior commitments to a method, the compelling logic of the problems leads to questioning. Those in the field have so frequently lost all perspective that discussion is impossible.

Some of the traditional controversy confusing and alienating parents and professional workers has been further complicated by a misunderstanding of the word *deafness*. To some, it implies total inability to hear. To others, it means a failure to understand the spoken word immediately. Some virtually deny the existence of deafness and employ the euphemism "hearing impaired." We have found it most meaningful to define deafness as *a loss of hearing sufficiently severe to render an understanding of conversational speech impossible in most situations with or without a hearing aid*. In this book, the phrase "severe and profound deafness" derives from this definition.

Although a child may perceive a drum beat, respond to a shout, or look up at an airplane passing overhead, he is psychologically, educationally, and socially deaf if he cannot understand speech. Destructive confusion and controversy has grown from a simple failure to realize that sound perception for random nonspeech noises does not allow an understanding of speech. Deafness so defined seems clear; it sounds logical and too obvious to need special explanation. The current condition of the rehabilitation commitment for the deaf shows that far more than simple definitions are needed. Common sense has been struck down by nonsense.

Over the first two years of the project, Dr. Vernon and I spent many hours discussing the various related issues. More and more, the necessity for a comprehensive statement on deafness and its ramifications grew obvious. The communication controversy must be considered in the whole context of family and community. Important issues are so diverse, their interrelationships so knotty, that brief, sometimes heated discussions almost never lead to resolution. Thus, around the middle of 1969, the idea for this book was born. There seemed only one appropriate way to consider all aspects of the problem — unite them between the covers of a book.

The book was initiated as a cooperative effort and has remained so throughout. Dr. Vernon's seventeen years of experience as psychologist, teacher, and above all, good friend to the deaf community echoes through this volume. Although five of seven chapters were authored by me, they were carefully reviewed by Dr. Vernon, who added the sensitive points that only experience and deep commitment make possible.

As our discussions developed, they ranged from the considerations of the individual child, to the nature of the professional and lay communities which have allowed a perpetuation of mythical notions as to "what is good for the deaf child." In the writing, there was a progressive broadening of the perspective; although knowledge gained from each of the individual areas which we examined seemed to hold promise for giving "the answer" to the resistance to needed changes, we were still left feeling that the "complete answer" had not been found. This feeling remained until we came to understand that answers to questions about deaf children can only be found in examining the whole of their life circumstances as an integrated process.

With the completion of the book, we are left with the unsettled feeling that understanding of the deaf community by the hearing community is limited. In our search, we have learned much about the hearing community, not only how it has dealt with deaf people by denying their unique needs and suppressing their difference, but how society at large tends to maintain itself by carefully controlling various groups that tend to disrupt its equilibrium. Deaf persons have been overcontrolled; the threat that deaf persons will be disruptive because of their differences is more imagined than real.

Perhaps many times as one reads this book, he will ask "Of what relevance is this or that issue?" What is contained here represents the authors' ideas of what issues are relevant. The relevance cannot always be explicitly documented; to do so, in each instance, would require many additional volumes. Our hoped-for result is that enough areas will seem relevant to enough people so that they can then develop the meaningfulness more than in the present effort.

Our traditional approach to understanding deaf people has been to look at areas in which they have failed, then to reasons for those failures. Originally, explanations centered around the idea that failures, especially educational failures, were intrinsically related to deafness. A series of psychological studies were published in support of that premise. Some still regard deaf children as intrinsically retarded and admonish parents to expect no more than fifth-grade academic achievement. Dr. Vernon has been one of the leaders in defeating this destructive idea through research, articles, and speeches. The deaf child's intelligence had originally been examined by using standard verbal intelligence tests. The baseline for comparison was the scores of hearing children. That the deaf child has a major sensory deficit precludes the use of such materials without careful and considered modification.

We are writing as psychiatrist and psychologist, but psychiatric and psychological aspects of deafness are only a part of the total problem. Paradoxically, despite their significance, they have probably received the least objective, scientific attention. There have been a few books covering these psychiatric and psychological phenomena, but when all of the categories of published material on deafness are compared for sheer volume, psychological works constitute only a small portion. Neither normative language development nor normative psychological development can be taken for granted in the deaf child. Normal patterns of language or psychological development do not adequately serve as baselines for behavior in the deaf child. One hope is that this book will help to clarify distinctions in linguistic and psychological development of deaf children.

Another hoped-for result of this effort is overcoming one of the chief obstacles to progressive development of services for deaf children. This is the failure to develop effective interactions and coalitions between parents and professionals. Parents of young deaf children seldom know or speak to the parents of older deaf children or to deaf adults. Communication between these groups is vital to the growth of a parent's understanding of deaf children. We want to help parents and professionals concerned with the deaf child to see the whole of the problem, not just bits and pieces related to this or that aspect of the problem; i.e., to see themselves and deaf children "in perspective."

One of the main complaints of deaf children and adults is the isolation they feel from their families and community. Such complaints are no less frequent from deaf people educated in traditional oral programs. We shall demonstrate why the many hours spent acquiring an oral technique do not necessarily establish feelings of closeness between human beings. Closeness comes from meaningful exchanges of information and feeling; in short, from understanding and empathy.

One of man's greatest assets is also one of his greatest liabilities: the capacity to probe and learn. We are made to learn, to grow, and to change. When this does not occur, we suffer. Just as our muscles become flabby and inefficient when we lie ill in bed, so our minds lie fallow when they are not allowed to function as they were intended.

The thought of being isolated from one's fellow human beings and from the sound environment in which we live is painful for all to contemplate. If we did not have to be isolated, if we could understand what the intentions of the other persons were, if we could explore the richness of their behavior, if we could delve into the world's literature, then the loss of hearing would not be so intense. But without adequate language, we cannot do these things. This is why deaf persons are isolated.

They grow in silence, but they need not grow alone. For centuries, the deaf have been one of nature's "experiments" on the effects of cultural isolation. But for all its years, this "experiment" has resulted in little to bring the deaf into the mainsteam as equals. When all of the academic and pseudo-academic rhetoric generated over how best to educate and socialize the deaf is over, they and they alone must live out the "results." The results, when examined honestly, are not encouraging. But by early appropriate intervention at the social and educational level today and tomorrow, the deaf child and his family need not continue to be strangers in the same house.

Foreword

The history of the involvement of the Institute for Psychosomatic and Psychiatric Research and Training of the Michael Reese Hospital and Medical Center in the psychosocial problems of deaf persons is somewhat complicated, but worth sketching. During the latter part of World War II, I was stationed at an air force rehabilitation center as chief of professional services. Stationed at a nearby air base, a young otologist, Dr. Robert Henner, also from Michael Reese Hospital, frequently visited me to talk about psychological problems in his field.

When we returned to our civilian duties, Dr. Henner raised funds and organized a Hearing and Speech Center just as I was planning and designing a Psychiatric Institute; both were opened at Michael Reese Hospital in 1951. Dr. Henner constantly pleaded with me for psychiatric help in his work. Unfortunately, we could spare no psychiatrist because we were attempting to build up a body of professionals in the decade of the 1950's for a just emerging field. Dr. Henner died in 1960 before we could cooperate with this pioneer who understood the immense psychological and psychiatric problems associated with early deafness.

In 1965, Dr. McCay Vernon became director of a planning survey at DePaul University to determine the possibility of a coordinated training program for professionals interested in working with persons handicapped by defects in speech and hearing. About the same time, Michael Reese received a donation for a free-standing Hearing and Speech Center to be named after the late Mr. David Siegel, in which the Dr. Robert Henner Hearing and Speech Center was to be the Diagnostic and Therapy section. Frequent conferences with members of the Social and Rehabilitation Service of the Department of Health, Education and Welfare (HEW) and others, a visit to the pioneering state mental hospital at Rockland, New York, where Drs. Alschuler and Ranier had initiated a unit for the study of deaf psychotics, stirred our own interest. We were able to obtain a three-year grant for the support of our work through the cooperation of Miss Mary Switzer and Drs. William Usdane and Boyce Williams. The grant was timed so that our pilot studies would be completed approximately when the Siegel Institute would be ready. The report of our work has been published: *Psychiatric Diagnosis Therapy and Research on the Psychotic Deaf* (supported by Department of Health, Education and Welfare Social Rehabilitation Service Grant Number RD-2407-S, Final Report, September 1, 1969 — Institute for Psychosomatic and Psychiatric Research and Training, Michael Reese Hospital and Medical Center, Chicago.)

We were fortunate to have in our working group not only professionals working with deaf adults* but also Dr. Eugene D. Mindel, a child

---

*D. Rothstein, M.D., G. Joosten, M.D., Harry Easton, Ph.D., J.D. Koh, Ph.D., L.L. Collums, M.A., and a number of consultants and technicians.

psychiatrist, and Dr. Vernon, a clinical psychologist, who were interested in working with deaf children and their families. This book is the result of their labors and contains not only the data from their investigations but also ideas, suggestions, and conclusions about educational processes important for the families and professionals working with deaf children: pediatricians, psychologists, psychiatrists, social workers, and teachers.

An inadequate understanding of the problems of the deaf abounds in the literature and in the pronouncements of professionals, especially educators. The deaf are not dumb in the sense of having lesser or poor capacity for abstraction, for intellectual development, or education. They are indeed handicapped, but made worse by biased concepts of teaching motivated toward maintaining traditional methods encrusted in professional "establishments."

A concerted effort should be directed toward the enlightenment of the families of deaf children to facilitate opportunities for proper education before critical periods are reached, after which adequate education is difficult if at all possible. So many family and marital problems need to be understood: the stress of the deaf child on the family, grandparents' interference, denial of deafness, rationalizations, hostility, and confused or delayed decisions. The natural impact of the discovery of deafness is shock, hostility, guilt, empathic coddling, social isolation, et cetera. It is only when grief, anger, guilt, and helplessness are resolved that steps are taken to facilitate the teaching of adequate means of communications: manual (signing) plus whatever oral systems are appropriate.

The wide variety of reactions depend on the personality of the parents, the cause of deafness (hereditary, measles, Rh+ factor, prematurity, et cetera) and the degree of deafness. Therefore, early examination for brain damage and early audiological studies are necessary. When the results are known, families can be helped through individual and group therapy and the children dealt with by appropriate psychological and educational methods. Thereby behavioral disturbances that could cripple the deaf child for all of his life can be avoided, and the family can be at peace with itself.

The authors discuss all these problems in detail. In language understandable to the average family, they present cogent arguments for their recommendations and thereby contribute a significant optimistic prediction for the deaf child to grow into a healthy adult who can work well and not underachieve, love well, play well, and socialize with his peers and continue to be optimistic for a good life. This important book may stir angry controversy among those who traditionally fight for unproven assertions, but it tells a story for those who really want to know.

Roy R. Grinker, Sr., M.D.
Director of the Institute
Professor of Psychiatry
Michael Reese Hospital
and Medical Center
Chicago, Illinois.

Acknowledgments

The various individuals whose counsel we invited in understanding deaf children and adults and whose advice we sought in the preparation of the actual text all share a common interest. All have worked to bring about a more meaningful rapprochement between deaf people and the hearing community at large. There is some divergence of opinion among them on how best to accomplish this goal. Thus, not all share all of the views expressed in this book. We wish to acknowledge the contribution each has made.

First and foremost, we want to express our appreciation to Dr. Roy R. Grinker, Sr., who included us as colleagues in the rich intellectual climate that has characterized the Institute for Psychosomatic and Psychiatric Research and Training, Michael Reese Hospital and Medical Center, Chicago, for its many years under his directorship. Dr. Grinker served as the chief investigator of the Project for the Deaf, supported by a research and demonstration grant (RD-2407-S) from the Division of Research and Demonstration Grants, Social and Rehabilitation Service, Department of Health, Education and Welfare. Over the Project's three years, 1966 to 1969, he guided our thoughts into a deep understanding of the effects of isolation on psychological development.

There were several other key members of the project team. Dr. David Rothstein and Dr. George Joosten, who both worked with the adult deaf patients, contributed psychodynamic insights to our understanding of deaf people. Dr. Harry Easton, and Dr. Soon Duc Koh, as the clinical psychologist and research psychologist, respectively, each added a particular dimension of psychological insight to our group.

Miss L. L. Collums participated on the project as the psychiatric social worker. Her contribution to this book stands apart from participation in the research group as a whole. Miss Collums meticulously read the entire text. Her sensitivity profoundly influenced its final form. She, as many professionals working with the deaf, is the child of deaf parents and was able, therefore, to heighten our awareness of some key areas of interest to deaf people.

Three other individuals aided in the preparation of the total text. Mrs. Ethyl Untermeyer shared freely of her experiences in rearing her deaf son, Abraham. She gave us permission to include her experiences with Abraham as an integral part of the text. She and two of our original editors, Mr. and Mrs. Marion Reis, brought into sharper focus some of the poignancy of their roles as parents of deaf children. Mrs. Bonnie Litowitz read the text from the psycholinguistic standpoint. We have been very interested in stimulating studies by the psycholinguistic community on the development of the deaf child's language. We feel her specific paper, summarized in the text, is an important step in that direction.

Much of the contact with deaf children and their parents occurred in the Henner Hearing and Speech Center, Dr. Laszlo Stein, Director. The

Henner Center, now part of the David T. Siegel Institute for Communicative Disorders, contains an educational program specifically for young deaf children. This grew out of the preschool nursery for deaf children, which was established by Dr. Stein and conducted by Miss Marianne Collins and Miss Alice Moss. Miss Collins and Miss Moss, coming from pediatric audiology and deaf education, respectively, had become dissatisfied with traditional approaches to deaf children and found the freedom to develop their own ideas and share them with others in the environment of Michael Reese. Many of our insights on deaf children and their families were developed through our associations with these two teachers. In addition, Miss Collins and Miss Moss served as readers and critics of chapters five and six, representing areas of their special competence. Not all of the views represented in these chapters are necessarily completely shared by them. In general, however, their dedication and interest in deaf children subtly found expression in various portions of this book.

Dr. Laszlo Stein, the Director of the David T. Siegel Institute, has been involved with the project and with the nursery school from the outset and contributed freely of his knowledge as an audiologist and researcher. Chapter four was read by him in its several preliminary versions; he patiently struggled with the authors in shaping it into a more understandable statement. Dr. Darryl Rose also read and contributed to the final shape of chapter four. His statement that "these things need to be said" helped to carry us through the difficult times encountered in its writing.

Our deepest gratitude is to the parents of deaf children. It is to them that we have really devoted this book. Our concerns over the unresolved agonies of these parents was the guiding stimulus throughout its writing. There are now too many parents to mention by name. We wish, however, to present this book as a gift in return for what they have given to us. They have enriched not only our understanding of deaf children and adults, but our understanding of the various ways in which families cope with severe stress.

We are fortunate in Illinois in having an active and articulate association of deaf people—The Illinois Association of the Deaf, an affiliate of the National Association of the Deaf. Our contacts with Mr. J. B. Davis, Mr. Samuel Block, and Mr. Robert Donaghue have imbued us with the deaf man's views. Mr. Frank Sullivan, President of the National Fraternal Society of the Deaf, also located in Chicago, has widened our contacts with and understanding of deaf people.

Behind the scenes, one always felt the helpful presence of Dr. Boyce Williams, Chief, Communications Section, Social and Rehabilitation Services. Dr. Williams, himself a deaf man, has been the guiding force, the "angel," for so many projects most sensitive to the actual needs of deaf people.

There are two women, teachers of sign language, who have worked tirelessly toward implementing what they feel is appropriate for and the right of deaf children. Both are children of deaf parents. In 1966, Mrs. Kay Munro established a sign language class at Michael Reese Hospital and in the northwest suburbs of Chicago. The latter continues to operate and is open to any person who wishes to attend. It provides a meeting ground for a cross section of people with varying interests in deaf people—from concerned grandparents to ballet teachers interested in the physical development of deaf children. The numerous social functions arranged by Mrs. Munro and her friends provided a meeting ground for deaf adults, deaf adolescents, deaf children, and hearing parents and grandparents. At the conclusion of the project in 1969, over two-hundred parents had participated in that program. Mrs. Candy Haight has worked in a north suburban school district in implementing a simultaneous program for deaf children. Her sensitivities and knowledge have insured the success of that program. Both women also served as sign language teachers to the parents of the Henner Preschool Nursery Program.

Over the past few years, we have been welcomed into several institutions serving the needs of deaf children. These contacts have been richly rewarding, and although there are some philosophical differences, nonetheless, one cannot help but admire the single-minded devotion to helping deaf children. Among those visited were: The John Tracy Clinic in Los Angeles, where discussions were freely held with Mrs. Spencer Tracy, Dr. Edgar Lowell, Dr. Althena Smith, and Mrs. Thielman; The California School for the Deaf at Riverside, Dr. Richard Brill, Superintendent, which has pioneered in developing flexible approaches to the education of deaf children; The Wisconsin School for the Deaf, under the leadership of Mr. Kenneth Huff; and the Jewish Vocational Services of Chicago, which conducts a workshop program for deaf adolescents and adults.

Our three secretaries: Mrs. Judith Booth, Mrs. Rosita Materre, and Mrs. Josephine Wright, all painstakingly deciphered and transformed into legibility the initial thoughts represented in this book.

Finally, we wish to thank our families who have graciously accepted the severe impositions on time rightfully theirs over the two years of the writing of this book.

Chapter 1

The Hearing Man's Bias

Much of the current lore and literature of deafness revolves about one central idea: a deaf person without speech is virtually helpless! Torrents of words supporting this assumption have effectively drowned out any voice of protest. The findings of the few extensive methodological investigations into the real difficulties created by severe and profound deafness are largely overlooked.

One who reads literature about deafness discovers that many prescriptions for deaf persons serve not them but the people serving the deaf.[1] Teachers of the deaf often use their own projected feelings in attempting to understand the plight of their deaf students; facts are ignored.[2] The primary problems of those born deaf are not caused just by inarticulate speech. Serious problems are frequently caused by their inability to ascertain subtler aspects of human behavior. These subtle aspects play an important role as articulate speech develops in the normal-hearing child. What is seldom understood, and even more rarely applied, is that talking out loud is just a small part of human communication.

We hearing individuals easily misconceive the significance of speech. We use ourselves as a natural frame of reference. Because we talk out loud and consciously think inside with that same voice (or so it seems), we assume the appropriate educational stance is to help the deaf child develop this same capacity. This approach assumes that our own speaking and thinking processes can be duplicated in the deaf by teaching them speech and speech reading. Speech developed as a common channel of communication for those of us who hear, but countless mental and physical activities contributed to its development, and these constitute the real substance of language.

During childhood, the hearing individual's capacity to monitor what he said and heard was extremely important in his language development. This capacity contributed first to the sound of his speech and later on to meaning. The sounds monitored were recorded in the brain along with contextual associations, to be drawn upon later in order to produce, clarify, and enrich communication. In addition, as speech and language developed, emotional mechanisms cast good or bad feelings on what was heard and said. These feelings later operated as censors and influenced what was said and what was not said.

There is a compelling desire to hear ourselves talk, which could easily lead us far astray, babbling nonsensically into eternity were it not for a fortunate occurrence—fellow man. As much as we like to hear ourselves talk, fellow man does not always like to listen. He, too, likes to hear himself talk. There are effective and well-known methods for shutting off fellow man. Thus the hearing man monitors not only his own speech but the reactions of others to what he says. This adds the social dimension to speech.

The average hearing man usually thinks of a deaf person as one who once was a hearing individual with fully developed language who then became deaf. It is on this assumption that the hearing man reflects. "What is it like?"

This attempt at intellectual empathy does not duplicate what the deaf person really experiences. The inner voice that carries the nondeaf through an intellectualized deafness is not present in the deaf individual. Instead, there is a symbolic language based on visual lip images, facial expressions, partly comprehensible gestures, and some formal fingerspelled words. Also included will be some formal and some homemade sign language and other sensory data related to touch, pain, smell, and so on. The bulk of this symbolic mass is probably composed of visual memories, often without sufficient language to communicate about them. Attempts to communicate with those who hear, using this unconventional language system, summarizes much of the deaf person's struggle in the hearing world about him.

We have attempted to depict two mental perspectives—the hearing person thinking about communication problems of the deaf person and the deaf person's thinking using his own language system. Learning to understand the nature of his language system is the task that befalls the deaf child's hearing parents. Much of the intent of this book is to convert the natural bias of the hearing parents into a realistic and constructive understanding of the implications of severe and profound deafness. This understanding is necessary for coping effectively with the special needs of the deaf child.

Why is it, then, that hearing people find it so difficult to understand why deaf people cannot develop a conventional language system? A sufficient answer should be that they do not acquire language in the conventional way. However, logic has not sufficed to explain why hearing individuals do not correctly conceive the implications of severe and profound hearing loss. We can offer three relevant considerations. First, most hearing individuals have had little or no meaningful contact with deaf children or adults.[3] Unfortunately, this is also true of many professionals in deaf education and rehabilitation, whose views are based on circumscribed contacts in the office or classroom.[4] Second, many people are unwilling to accept the implications of deafness because it is unpleasant to do so. And third, many persons closely associated with deaf people remain loyal to educational systems that support an unwillingness to believe the real outcomes of deafness. This is especially true in systems where the teaching of speech and speech reading is upheld as the only appropriate pedagogical technique.

Mannerisms of Deaf People That Support the Bias

Some mannerisms of deaf persons support the disavowal of reality. All hearing people who have worked with deaf people have observed their smiling and attentive appearance. Hearing people interpret this in several ways. Superficially, they may comment that the deaf child or adult is a "very happy" or "very pleasant" person. These are usually innocuous observations made by someone who previously has not spoken to a deaf person but has overcome his reluctance long enough to make a casual observation. When the deaf person smiles, it usually means he has chosen to conceal his embarrassment and dismay at not being a full participant in the conduct of human affairs. Thus, he gets the hearing person and himself "off the hook." The deaf person has discovered only too often that to say "what" or to ask for an explanation results in the hearing person's anger, impatience, or rejection. This is not an indictment: that we all bear collective guilt for the communicative vacuum into which the deaf have been placed. Most hearing people, however, do not choose to become involved with the deaf because it is often too frustrating.

We know that early in an infant's life, the smile becomes a significant means of effecting and sustaining social contact. The smile is central to early communication between mother and child. The smiles of an infant occur within the caretaking milieu when speech is not yet important. To engage in some fanciful speculation, one could consider that the deaf person's smile is partially an attempt to recapture a bit of the benign and mostly gratifying experiences of infancy—an endeavor to translate the absence of human contact into the mood of a time when verbal communication was not a necessity.

Perhaps this early automatic smile is never lost in order to compensate for interpersonal contact. However, the smile of the deaf adult can deceive both the deaf and hearing person. For the hearing person, the deaf person's smile is often a deception because he mistakes it for contentedness or comprehension. For the deaf person, it is a deception because it does not force the hearing person to make a greater effort to communicate with him. Thus, the deaf person is deprived of further contact and additional knowledge.

Here it must be emphasized that we refer to a hearing person who speaks to a deaf person without gestures, sign language, or fingerspelling. This is most often the case. Few people outside the deaf establishment— the deaf, their family, teachers, and friends—know the language of signs. Even within the deaf establishment, speech is often the forced mode of communication.

Educational Philosophies

An educational system has been built in part on the natural reactions described above. It is an educational system that generally forces deaf people to conform to an image of what hearing people think they should be. The "model" deaf man is hewn from the hearing man's image of himself. An inability to hear renders the full execution of this image impossible under any circumstances; the attempt is pursued nonetheless.

Once having discovered their child's deafness, parents naturally wish to help the child have what they believe will be a "normal" life. If they are led to believe that methods exist to do so, they will eagerly embrace and support them. It is not until too late that the parents come to another painful realization: *teaching speech and speechreading alone will not develop articulate speech or adequate language comprehension.*

As any parent of a deaf child taught by oral methods and any teacher of oralism knows, teaching children by this method is difficult and frustrating.[5] For this reason, deaf education is not a field with wide popular appeal. For teachers of deaf children, the reward, word acquisition, accrues slowly. It is measured in days or months, in painful comparison to the hearing child whose new words and language forms develop too rapidly to be measured. There must be special motivation, other than money, for entering this field, since comparable salaries and opportunities are available in other fields of special education.

Given the difficulties inherent in teaching deaf children, the difficulties in recruiting a full complement of teachers and staff, and the failure of current methods, it would seem there should be room for recent comers with fresh, divergent ideas. This attitude, however, does not characterize the present state of deaf education. Inbreeding, pedantry, and narrowness of view, authoritarianism and paternalism mark the philosophies of the various parent and professional groups.[6]

Though one finds gradual shifts and slippage in the traditional views, a comprehensive outside perspective of the field gives the impression that in the development of new insights and methods an arrest has occurred. This is an appearance many oral educators would like to perpetuate; for the implication is, "We have all the answers" (see chapter 6). If young educators in the field have doubts, and many do, they will seldom stand to be heard. The pressures against speaking out are too great if one questions the prevailing philosophy. This may well imperil their professional future. But who suffers? The deaf child.

The questions of an enlightened parent are not welcome. Oral educators are often hostile to relevant questions regarding the efficiency of their techniques.[7] Their professional journal excludes papers representing opposing views.[8] But does this hostility not in fact carry with it the implicit notion that the educators are above reproach; that their methods are so refined and successful that they can not be questioned?

More often than not, parents are overwhelmed by this initial rebuff and the pretentions of the educators. Their initial questions about the effectiveness of this laborious method are often squelched. Usually they are told that they are not professionals and should leave all the decision making to the educators. They may be appointed as stand-in teachers, and later when the method fails—when the child cannot communicate as promised—there are implications and accusations that they are unfit as parents. There is never an open acknowledgment or an honest appraisal that the educational techniques have failed. Parents who wish to adopt an alternative method such as the combined manual-oral method are challenged and intimidated. They and their children are labeled "oral failures". Parents who have used this method or have inquired about it are often threatened that their child will not be accepted into a regular public or parochial school program that follows the oral method.

It is at this point of challenge that a significant test of rights occurs. Is it not a perversion of the democratic process that has allowed a group of adherents to a particular form of classroom instruction to so dominate this field that they can threaten to and do exclude children of parents who use this method? An extreme example is in the state of Massachusetts, where a group of ambitious oral educators succeeded in convincing the Massachusetts Legislature to pass a law disallowing the use of manual communication in the classroom. This is akin to passing a law that would prevent the use of Hebrew in Jewish Schools. Paradoxically, the most influential educators who impose oralism upon public schools and who dominate professional and governmental organizations are often themselves in expensive private institutions. Because parents have been convinced by oral educators that this is the only method, no pressure is brought to bear to test the constitutionality of such laws and procedures.

There is often so much politics and factionalism among parent, teacher, and administrative groups that the needs of deaf children are overlooked. They become pawns to systems that are acting more for the benefit of professionals and parents than deaf children.[9] Yet deaf children and to some extent deaf adults by virtue of their educational and communication problems are ill equipped to protest the system. Typically their protests against the ineptitude of their educators are shunned. Deaf children protest their frustration with their bodies: they throw tantrums or hit or bite or utter loud noises that sound more like the babbling of the very young than the speech of children their age. Their protest only brings them grief — and the impervious establishment maintains its repressive inertia.

Deafness and General Education

Educational goals for deaf children have been derived from goals originally developed for hearing children. Even textbooks for hearing children are used; though they may have sections about the telephone, public speaking, singing, et cetera. Many educational prescriptions for deaf and hearing children have been empirically conceived and empirically proved to fail but are clung to nonetheless. These prescriptions are imbedded in and promoted by a variety of catch phrases, the most frequent of which are "every child deserves the chance for an oral education," and "a deaf child is just like any other child except he is deaf," which a person with the appropriate knowledge quickly relegates to their rightful place — obscurity.

Deaf children do not necessarily learn on the same schedule as hearing children. They must devote their energies to extracting subtleties from the environment that hearing children perceive through hearing. Five-and-six-year-old deaf children are often made endlessly to repeat letter copying drills and recite by rote sentences that serve to create the impression of conventional language learning.

Why have we allowed such a situation to develop in deaf education? It is due in part to our placing material priorities above welfare priorities so that many slipshod practices for dealing with handicapped persons easily develop and pass unnoticed. Beyond this, however, much of deaf education represents a microcosm of our general educational and political system. Most of us were also cramped into a classroom niche in a desk and chair bolted to the floor. This unnatural cage that we all so early allowed ourselves to be thrust into symbolized the natural limits imposed on our mind's pursuits. To get up and explore the surroundings or spontaneously communicate with one's neighbor was regarded as a threat to the prevailing order. In such stuffy classrooms, seeds of ideas dry up for want of fertile fields. A little sun gets through here and there, but mostly we are trained to become trivia's yeomen.

Chapter 2

The Impact of the Deaf Child on His Family

In the following pages we will examine the development of the deaf child and his family from the point when suspicions first develop that the child is disabled, through the confrontation with the fact of his deafness at the time of definitive diagnosis, to the time beyond, when he and his family must adjust to his disability and make appropriate life decisions for him.

Until the present time, deaf children, other disabled children, and their families have been considered primarily in a number of narrow, parochial frameworks. Professional and conceptual separation have been maintained between groups of relevant professional personnel. For example, most programs for deaf children do not adequately provide for the emotional needs of the parents, thus limiting the success of the child and his total education. This situation has led to greater rather than lesser confusion in services provided for the deaf child and his family.

In this chapter, we are attempting to give parents and professionals a full and accurate perspective of the total social and psychological system in which they participate. The continuing failure to recognize all aspects of the system has not eliminated their relevance. Unrecognized significant aspects of any system will surface regardless; and because their influence is not acknowledged, they can act as obstacles to the successful growth of the total plan. There are educational systems that fail to consider the early need for distinct and clear communication between parent and child. This will restrict the educational and emotional outcome from the onset. Hence, parents must be fully informed early in their deaf child's life of all the ramifications of deafness.

The discovery of the child's deafness is not an event that happens instantly. It feels as if this happens all at once because the emotional reaction becomes so intense when the parent is finally confronted with reality. The discovery, however, is a gradual unfolding of knowledge about the child. This unfolding depends on many factors. One of these is the natural history of diseases causing deafness. They will be discussed separately in the next chapter. Those that will be considered here are the nature of the parents' personalities; the state of the marriage; the parents' relationship to members of the extended family; the ordinal position of the deaf child; and the importance of verbal language to the family and culture. Some of these factors retard discovery of the deafness, while others more directly force awareness upon the parents.

The Influence of the Parents' Personalities

The parent's individual personality influences significantly the initial perception of the child's deafness. This is a pivotal issue, for the same personality traits that figure in the discovery of the deafness will influence crucial decisions that parents make later for the child. If the discovery is prolonged by denial and rationalization beyond the time when obvious behavioral patterns in the infant reveal the deafness, then we would expect that future parental decisions, which require shifts in emphasis or orientation, will occur slowly and thus beyond the optimum time. Such delays are destructive to deaf children and their families. In a child's development there are optimum periods for learning.[1] When the growing child passes through and beyond ideal periods without having had the opportunity for learning, the delay often results in an irreversible loss. This is especially true in language learning and all that is dependent upon it.[2]

In discussing parents' personalities, we will describe personality in terms of its adaptive capacities that define an individual's ability to cope with unanticipated occurrences. This is in contrast to the conventional approach of discussing several separate personality functions, then relating to the general problem.

By studying an individual's ways of responding to novel and unusual situations at different points in the process of his growth and maturity, we are able to determine his capacity to adapt to life generally. By considering his capacity to adapt in this context, we avoid the nonproductive intellectual trap of judging "normality" versus "abnormality". Such labels force us to make universal judgments; whereas an examination of adaptive capacity permits a study of an individual within the framework of particular situations.

Here we are specifically interested in ascertaining the capacity of parents to deal with the unanticipated occurrence of having a deaf child. A necessary step in this direction is understanding the life history of the individual parent. One can examine a parent's history for various episodes of greater-than-average stress; for example, the various difficulties inherent in the period when the parent as a child entered kindergarten. If this revealed a history of social withdrawal or a loss of emotional control, one might expect a compromised capacity to cope.

Adaptive capacities will differ between the mother and father primarily on the basis of male versus female orientation. Although we realize that such a dichotomy introduces artificiality, nonetheless the coping mechanisms of mothers and fathers are sufficiently different in rearing young children that we feel it is a valid distinction to discuss.

During gestation, the mother psychologically regards the fetus as part of her own body. She projects onto the fetus the many fears, expectations and other emotions derived from her own childhood. Many of the mother's thoughts during childbearing are directed toward the nurturing environment that she proposes to provide for the child. Such thoughts are especially prominent with the first child. There is hopefulness for the child's future. Parents who have come from troubled homes and recall stressful times in their childhood often take an optimistic vow: "With my child, it will be different."

Moreover, feelings related to the current marital situation can also influence the way in which the mother regards her child. If the marriage is not happy, anger can be displaced from the husband to the child *in utero* rather than directly to the husband. It would be more appropriate, of course, for the mother to handle this situation explicitly with her husband.

If at the time of birth, the newborn shows no obvious physical abnormalities, the infant and his mother enter into a relationship in which her expectations and feelings for the infant blend with his infant personality. As the infant's initial repertory of actions is mostly instinctual and not greatly different from other infants, the mother's reactions and interpretations of his behavior are based on her own personality. However, infants do differ in their evident endowment at birth. Some are very placid and easily cared for; others are irritable and difficult to please. The manner in which the parent deals with an uncomfortable infant is one measure of her ability to cope with her own frustrations. The newborn infant crying in hunger, pain, or fatigue can trigger strong emotions such as rage in the mother and blur her objectivity toward the child.

The mother's anger derives in part from her inability to easily determine the sources of the child's discomfort. With the deaf child, however, a similar situation continues long beyond the period of infancy. Under ordinary circumstances, the deaf child is not given adequate methods to communicate important feelings at an early age.

In the mother's role as a provider and as a buffer between the infant and his surroundings, she finds certain of the child's approaches and assaults on the environment are acceptable and others unacceptable. For example, some mothers enjoy a small boy's aggression; they see it as harmless. As the aggressive toddler moves about in his home, occasionally damaging prized items, they accept his behavior. Other mothers become enraged by the aggression, see it as "bad," and will readily punish the child.

Similarly, the child's affectionate advances will be placed on a scale of values: a child's affection can be regarded as "too much" or "not enough." The mother's attitudes are of particular importance during the first year of life because it is she who is most often with the infant. The father may rarely be home when the baby is awake. Later, the child's personality development will come under the influence of both father and mother. Yet, the mother's personality will have considerably more influence on the kind of environment that is presented to the child.

The deaf child, because he must depend more often on communication of a nonverbal nature, remains more dependent on the mother than the normally hearing child. His is a forced dependence born of an inability to develop conventional communication. This inability forces him to depend on the actions, not the words, of the few people with whom he is familiar. He must approach strangers cautiously. Often they provide little or no novel learning opportunity for him, for rarely can they handle with ease the difficulties inherent in activities and communication with a deaf child. Few are comfortable in playing appropriate games with deaf children.

Because the deaf child has a severely restricted choice of people from whom he can learn, what the mother regards as acceptable and unacceptable will be more firmly implanted as a permanent part of the deaf child's personality pattern.

The deaf child's forced dependence upon the mother imposes additional frustrations on her. She cannot extricate herself physically or emotionally from the care of the child through outside activities. Even a working mother, who has provided for the child's normal daytime activities (school or baby-sitting arrangements), must forego a day's employment when the child becomes ill or must be taken for some special examination. The child's needs are primary. Some mothers view this situation as burdensome and intolerable.

From the father's side of it, as we examine a man's life history, we should note the aggressive* ways he meets those challenges of his development that require him to make adjustments. A discussion of his own adolescent male patterns in dating, in school, and in sports is particularly revealing. This can lead to an understanding of the father's interpretation of his child's deafness. For a male, an aggressive approach to adolescence with many successes would be indicative of greater adaptive capacity, *but* it would also influence the father's conception of what his deaf son should accomplish. His self-image as a male projects an ideal of successful action with aggressive handling of impediments. Yet, a deaf boy to a certain extent is forced into a passivity unnatural for a male. The use of language, with maturity, serves aggressive ends; we can substitute words for direct action. That is, we can speak in a forthright manner but do not have to act that way. A common problem with deaf males is impulsive, nonconstructive aggression.[3] Its roots are easily seen in their inability to use language to channel their frustration and aggression.

Fathers often become more concerned with the future implications of the child's deafness. It is they who traditionally earn the family's support and shoulder the accompanying frustrations. A father will wonder how his deaf son can function as an adult with complex responsibilities. The father may see deafness as meaning a lack of capacity to compete successfully in obtaining hard currency and security. With a deaf daughter, a father may be more concerned about her safety, especially as the girl moves closer to puberty. He questions her capacity to distinguish good versus bad intent in others.

The Deaf Child's Family

Although the parents' individual personalities are important in relation to the deaf child, so too are their collective personality factors, which will result from and be modified and influenced by the marriage relationship. As the marriage evolves, it tends to take on certain characteristics dependent upon the parents' personalities. A marriage is a human system initially comprised of two separate individuals. Eventually it assumes and contains characteristics resulting from the interactions of the two personalities and the acquired memories of their shared life experiences.

The relationships parents had with their own mothers and fathers

---

*Aggression as used here does not imply destructive aggression. What is meant is the male thrust through definitive constructive action.

will have considerable influence on the nature and effects of the marriage. What parents experienced as children in their own home provides the expectations and patterns of behavior in their marriage. This is illustrated by the clinical observation that separations and divorces often occur in families where similar occurrences had taken place between the partners' parents. Family conflicts tend to be reenacted in succeeding generations. If these conflicts are severe and nonadaptive, greater disturbance can occur in the offspring than was evident in the parents or grandparents.

In assessing the capacities of a couple to deal with the stresses that evolve in the course of their marriage, our present concern is the reaction to the stress of having a noncommunicative child or a child who will never communicate conventionally. Some background information will be helpful in approaching this material.

As indicated earlier, each parent has built-in expectations for his or her child. As a child develops the ability to communicate, the parent can transmit these expectations using conventional speech. Some expectations can be communicated without speech. The child analyzes his environment and learns the "house rules." Some rules are interpreted more liberally than others. Absolute "must nots" will often be emphasized by physical punishment. Lesser prohibitions will be treated more liberally. This ambiguity can lead to confusion for the deaf child. *Ambiguity in communication is one of the deaf child's greatest problems in the home.* For him even more than for the hearing child, reasonable expectations must be clearly defined. If the parents' expectations continually vary—yesterday, it was okay with father to tear up the evening paper, but not okay with mother, and today it's okay with mother—this will cause perplexity and confusion for the deaf child. If this happens often, the deaf child will tend more and more to restrict his activities to avoid stressful states of confusion and anxiety. He will tend to limit his activities to those he knows to be safe and predictably acceptable to his parents. Eventually, his emotional and social growth will be restricted.

Ideally, the parents should function as a consistent unit in the formation of "house rules." When they do not, when they establish rules independently, this adds further confusion to the deaf child's environment. Ambiguity can occur because many situations in the marriage develop automatically and nonverbally. By mere observation, a husband or wife may intuit the partner's attitude toward the deaf child's behavior. Thus, open disagreement may be suppressed. Yet it is impossible to discuss explicitly the range of parental attitudes about the child's various activities. Often, it is only those actions of the child that stimulate conflict in the parents that are discussed between them; many times even these actions are not discussed. The parents' mutual capacity to deal with their disagreement over expectations and ideals will determine how successful they will be in handling the difficult situations that arise in the management of their deaf child.

The deaf child contributes additional confusion and conflict to a marriage. Rarely is either parent experienced in rearing a deaf youngster; nor do they know other parents of deaf children. They often struggle over their decisions for appropriate action in ignorance or with misinformation and may displace their frustrated feelings onto each other. Those marital conflicts stimulated by a deaf child that cannot be solved successfully have ramifications far beyond the child's problems and affect the entire marriage. Parents may thereby be thwarted in achieving anticipated parental and marital gratifications. However, when parents can mutually redirect their expectations and appreciate their deaf child's conforming to real rather than imagined capacities, they will achieve much satisfaction.

Is the Deaf Child the First Child?

A significant factor influencing the time of discovery of a child's deafness is his position in the sibship. With a first child, the mother does not know what to expect as a response to sound. With later children, the now-more-sensitive and observing mother has drawn up a mental schedule of expected growth and development. Though the schedule is in her mind, it is rarely expressed except in discussions with the pediatrician, family, or friends. Thus, the experienced parent suspects deafness sooner in the child who does not respond to the mother's voice at three months by cooing, who does not search for voices at four months, who later is not calmed by or responsive to sound, or whose first words do not occur on schedule.

The Extended Family

The nature of the parents' ties to their parents will exert considerable influence on the handling of the deaf child. The initial discovery of the deafness will be effected by the relationship of the deaf child's parents with his grandparents. From them, his parents have derived their own ideals about parenthood as well as ideals of social and professional achievement. Attitudes arising from these ideas are deeply imbedded and influence behavior automatically. Parents first discovering deafness may see themselves as failing to achieve a desired goal for their child. When parents perceive their failure to achieve a desired goal, their disappointment and concern will thread its way back to the ever-present question, "What will our own mothers or fathers think?" If the deaf child's parents sense failure, doubts and worries will develop. If, in contrast, they realize that they have lived up to the standards consonant with their ideals, a feeling of success and optimism can prevail.

In typical relationships between grandparents and parents, such concerns and attitudes flow naturally. If young parents having strong ties with the grandparents have a parent-child relationship rather than an adult-adult relationship, the interaction can be more stressful than gratifying. In such a relationship young parents still look to their own parents for reassurance and confirmation in achieving a position in life. Reassuring help is usually sought in the various decision-making situations that arise. Others feel that they have failed when they need to make such requests of the grandparents. This creates anger that can permeate most of the mutual contacts. Psychiatric theory refers to such situations between parents and grandparents as hostile-dependent relationships. On the other hand, where parents and grandparents have reached an agreement as to their proper roles, the relationship tends to be warm and comfortable because of the mutual recognition and respect for their appropriate positions. These parents can turn to the grandparents for guidance when they feel the latter's experience will contribute to the direction of their own lives.

With this as a frame of reference, we now consider the deaf child within the extended family group. When it is first suspected that the child cannot hear, one of the many concerns that will cross the parents' minds is the effect this may have on the relationships with their own parents. We have observed frequently that grandparents and some well-meaning friends will reinforce the parents' own wishful thinking with such statements as, "What you see and think to be true is probably not true." This is an ill-conceived effort to shield the parents from their feelings about having a deaf child. In saying this the grandparents are also trying to shield themselves. In identifying with their son or daughter, they attempt to shield themselves from the feelings provoked by this fact of deafness. The grandchild is seen as an extension of their own child, and hence an extension of themselves. Thus, the psychological problems do not affect family members in isolation, but because of the interplay of feelings in the family unit all members are affected in various ways.

The mother's new role is especially complex. After the use of early manual communication is suggested and begun, the mother will report that the grandparents are not supportive. She is willing to use it, knowing it will allow some reasonable communication between her and the child. The grandparents will discourage it because of their enduring conviction that things are not as they seem with the deaf child. Thus, to the mother befalls the tasks of being the first to accept the real state of the child, controlling her own feelings, educating the family as a whole, and accepting the brunt of all negative reactions.

All of these family pressures attempt to contradict the mother's realistic perception of her child's condition. Thus, an educational approach focusing on correcting the undeveloped speech is more palatable. This approach conforms to the consolations of grandparents and friends, who reassure the parents that the deaf child will eventually become like all other children.

Cultural Factors

We can discuss cultural factors only in a very general way. Our chief interest is understanding how cultural standards influence the original discovery of the child's deafness, especially the time and manner of the discovery.

Cultural and personality factors interrelate at practically all levels of an individual's life. Among persons of large families of limited educational background, the language development of the child does not usually rate a high premium. Other forms of behavior are used to determine whether the child is developing normally. Thus, the deafness may pass unnoticed until the child is three or even four years old. His symptomatic behavior, absence of speech, may be attributed to other causes: "He doesn't want to talk. He just doesn't listen. He is just stubborn!" These attitudes and reactions contrast with those of more educated groups, where great attention is given to articulation and to grammatical and semantic correctness. Earlier detection of deafness is more apt to occur when these concerns about language development are present.

When deaf children initially fail to respond to sound, it is not uncommon for them to be given corporal punishment by mistake. Later when the parent discovers the reasons for the child's failure to respond, much guilt occurs.[4] Parents who have had this unfortunate experience may need understanding and guidance from those sensitive to different values and priorities found in groups with varying socioeconomic backgrounds.

If the family has been under the care of a competent and experienced medical-center staff or private physician, the behavior indicative of deafness will usually be identified earlier and habilitative work can begin immediately. However, this is somewhat the ideal situation. The medical profession is not sufficiently enlightened about the behavioral manifestations of deafness in young children. Some physicians have been known to soothe fears with the concerned-grandparent reaction: "Everything will be all right; just give the child time."

Psychological Changes When Deafness is Discovered

When parents are confronted with the discovery of their child's deafness and finally realize that he is apparently not responding to environmental sounds, psychological operations come into play. These tend to prevent parents from becoming aware of things that cause them psychic pain. They experience blends of emotion interfering with their sense of well-being. Concerns lurk in the background and modify the typical emotional climate of the home, in which a child's spontaneity and innocence would usually create an air of hopefulness and pleasure. The dim awareness of their child's hearing loss has cast a shadow of doubt.

Dynamic psychiatry has identified a number of mechanisms by which human beings deal with stressful and unexpected occurrences. Many of these mechanisms are classified under adaptive behavior—the capacity of the individual to cope with the unanticipated. The more unique, complex, and stressful the occurrence, the more it taxes one's capacity for adaptive behavior. We will identify and describe aspects of this type of behavior in the following paragraphs.

When the evidence that her child is not hearing adequately becomes rationally incontrovertible, a mother experiences psychic pain. In contemplating this, she may allow herself to recognize the true nature of what is perceived; or, she may distort parts of what is perceived in such a way as to obscure the true picture. Thus, the question of the child's hearing loss may remain unanswered.

Denial and Rationalization

Two known psychological mechanisms by which reality is partially obscured are denial and rationalization. A mother may be able to perceive the true nature of a situation. However, in interpreting what she has perceived, she will exclude certain essential elements that would give the true picture of the child's hearing capacity. As our intellects lead us inexorably toward a painful realization, our feelings, stimulated by anticipated psychic pain, cause us to abandon or alter the nature of certain important perceptions so that the picture remains incomplete. Our initial reaction to emotional shock is disbelief. Disbelief eventually formalizes into denial.

Feelings can blur perception through a psychological denial that disregards certain essential elements of the child's total behavior. For example, a mother may ignore her observation that the child fails to respond to her voice. She sees the child turn as she approaches him while speaking. She lets herself interpret this as a response to her voice. She notices the child shift his gaze toward a door that has just been closed; she lets herself attribute this to a perception of sound rather than to the strong vibrations transmitted through the floor or the blocking of incoming light. The child may creep or crawl toward a television or hi-fi and put his ear very close. With residual hearing, he may even be alerted to loud environmental sounds such as the roar of a low-flying jet, the loud ringing of a doorbell, or the sharp bang of a slammed screen door. This does not mean that he can discern the crucial and more complex sound patterns of the human voice. In these examples, the mother denies the hearing loss by misinterpreting the significance of his responses to light, vibrations, or crude noises.

Another relevant psychological operation is rationalization. Rationalization creates fictionalized alternatives that replace the more realistic and pain-inducing explanations of the facts observed. Some rationalizations are culturally determined. Deafness may not immediately be seen as the reason for the child's unresponsiveness to sound. Instead, he is described as "just being stubborn" or "hearing what he wants to hear." Other reasons may be invoked such as a family history of "late talkers".

Where lack of hearing is *the* plausible explanation, the mother, as illustrated above, may use other factors concurrent in the environment to create an explanation other than deafness for the child's failure to hear. This is the essence of rationalization.

However long the period of denial and rationalization, parents will not obtain a more realistic understanding of their child until they bring him to a competent professional for definitive diagnosis. When professional opinion is finally rendered, and their fears that their child cannot hear are presumptively confirmed, they will experience what most parents call shock.

The Period of Shock

Regardless of the child's age, this period of shock follows the parents' confrontation with the fact of their child's deafness. The shock is a blend of disbelief and grief, helplessness, anger, and guilt. A person thrust into such a state suddenly feels set apart from the rest of society. The rest of the world, happier, content, and not burdened with grief passes by scarcely stopping long enough to notice the pains of others.

The disbelief the parent feels is a continuation of the earlier period of doubt. Gradually, as the acute grieving abates, the utter disbelief is supplanted by the question, "Why did it happen to me?" Some parents consciously regard the child's deafness as punishment for remembered transgressions; others feel it simply as punishment but are unable to perceive reasons. Some mothers recall fantasies of bearing a damaged child that they had when pregnant.

All expectant mothers have ambivalent feelings toward the growing fetus. Its birth and subsequent development promise gratification. The fetus derives unremittingly its share of nourishment and contributes increasingly to physical discomfort. Under stress, after discovering the child's disability, a mother may recall angry fantasies about the unborn child and mixed feelings about parenthood. She may associate these past feelings causally with the child's handicap and thereby feel responsible for the deafness. Intense feelings of guilt may ensue.

The dynamics and development of these feelings require explanation. Anger is a natural consequence of frustration and disappointment. Like all emotions, it seeks an object. Because of being disabled, the child may unfortunately be the object toward whom anger is directed. Although the mother consciously realizes the child has had no choice in his own destiny, she will, nonetheless, inexplicably find herself having negative feelings toward him. This in turn stimulates further guilt.

Anger originates from partial loss of maternal gratification in the first and second year of the deaf child's life. The mother's gratification normally arises from observing her baby's comfort after feedings. It increases in observing the child's attainment of growth and developmental milestones. If these satisfactions do not occur or are diminished, she feels hurt and inadequate. If they are attained, they confirm her success. The disabled child leaves the mother feeling only partially fulfilled as she looks for those accomplishments that are the rewards of her investment of time and love.

Anger also stems from the helplessness and confusion that come from not having anticipated a deaf child. The parents know little of what to expect or what to do. When they gradually realize the limitations imposed by deafness, they feel helpless because they cannot change it. As the child moves into his formative years for speech and language, the parent feels helpless in communicating basic information and conveying basic needs. They feel even more helpless when the child himself is fretting and can communicate only as much as squeals and tears and gestures will convey.

The mother experiences frustration trying to cope with a child whom she cannot understand and who cannot understand her. Moreover, she feels helpless in attempting to express her feelings sufficiently to gain relief from this seemingly irresolvable dilemma. Inevitably, those things seen as interfering with basic capacities to cope with the environment are likely to cause a sense of inadequacy. This too can stimulate anger. Thus, the presence of the deaf child in the family often causes unremitting frustration and anger. The causes of this are obscure to the casual observer.

Empathy and Overidentification

We tend to view other people through our own frames of reference. Thoughts and feelings about various people and situations that we impute to others are often projections of our own personality. These egocentric reactions color our perceptions of the life circumstances of others. Our perceptions that are marked by more objective and compassionate interpretations are said to show empathy. We are said to be empathic if it is within our capacity to assess another's position emotionally and intellectually. With our children, empathy is the most intense.

The child's development is influenced by the manner in which parents' thoughts and feelings contribute to the psychological structure of the home. Parents who only partially understand the true nature of the child's deafness, may over-identify with his position. For example, on viewing their child's situation subjectively, certain aspects will seem most stressful to them. They are said to be over-identifying with the child when they assume an inaccurate or exaggerated conception of the situation. In doing so they see the child's life circumstances more through their own frames of reference than through the child's. Over-identification is a pathological extension of empathy. Empathy implies a realistic appraisal of the disability. Those things that tend to interfere with basic capacities when coping with parent-child interactions are likely to stimulate anger in the child and the parents. The source of the parents' anger often is their over-identification. They have projected a concept of being a deaf child. This emphasizes the aspects of deafness that seem important to them because of their psychological needs. In contrast, the deaf child's anger has a different source, stemming from those situations when he wants to communicate and cannot.

Thus, a mother tends to perceive her child as an extension of herself. This is especially prominent in the earliest phases of the child's life. Even though the child has only the rudiments of an adult personality, she will tend to impute motivations that are in fact her own projections. Some of her pleasure comes in thinking how it would feel to be taken care of in the way that she is caring for him. Things that she perceives as hurtful or helpful, hating or loving, will be interpreted likewise for the child. If a part of the child is defective, the mother will think about this as she would experience it were it her loss. When doing this, she interprets her child's state as if she were suddenly deprived of the capacity to hear. The various fantasies related to the importance of hearing and associated unconscious psychological conflicts are projected as being the child's feelings. The projected fantasies may not be at all identical with the child's real feelings.

There are, then, two aspects of deafness with which the parent can either genuinely empathize or else over-identify. The first is the loss of hearing itself. Consciously and intellectually they can see the loss means not being able to get information that comes through hearing. Unconsciously, they may experience this loss more as a form of bodily injury. The second aspect is the social isolation consequent to the deafness.

Deafness as a Form of Bodily Injury

All of us develop sets of attitudes toward bodily injury. It is a universal reaction for a person to regard the loss of any body part as a diminution of his security.[5] He feels less secure because there is less equipment with which to adapt to stressful situations or enjoy pleasure-yielding opportunities. Some losses that are physically small are psychologically large. In part, the significance of a loss depends upon the age it is incurred. Children with early limb amputations experience self-consciousness and awkwardness. Psychologically they will regard this loss differently than an individual who has had a similar loss in his adolescence or beyond. At this point, the body part is not only an integral part of the individual's function in the physical sense, but it has also become invested with varieties of psychological meanings. Thus, with a loss at a later age, the individual gives up not only a part of himself, but must also alter psychological representations that have become a complete part of his self-concept and internalized body image.

Deafness is a far more complicated process than the loss of a body part. The child deaf from birth does not experience deafness as a loss in the sense of having had hearing. The parents, however, because of their empathic relationship experience the child's congenital deafness as a loss. From the outset, the congenital hearing loss will alter the nature of the child's contact with the world. Information that is obtained through the modality of hearing will be lost to him, leading to profound influences on his subsequent psychological and social development. As the deaf child becomes cognitively aware of the difference between himself and others between the ages of two and five and comes to understand that there is such a thing as hearing, he must reconcile his position. Even so, he does not experience this loss in the qualitative sense his parents do.

Deafness and Social Isolation

The second factor that the mother considers with her empathic relationship with her deaf child is the isolation imposed by deafness. The extent of this isolation is a matter of degree. With profound hearing loss, the child will be virtually excluded from information and human contact ordinarily available through hearing. This means the loss of that early mother-infant relationship conveyed through sound. During those early rudimentary communications between a mother and infant, the baby coos in response to its mother's voice. Since the human voice is a vehicle for feeling, the mother's vocalizing during the caretaking process is one way she communicates her tender feelings. Thus, varying degrees of deafness isolate the child from this tenderness in the mother's voice.

A more profound progressive isolation from the hearing world begins at the point when the child begins to depend upon auditory stimulation for the development of language and general knowledge. Residual hearing insufficient to allow the child to understand speech will isolate him from conventional language development and utilization. However, remnants of hearing may serve to alert him to the presence of other people and to loud environmental sounds. Hard-of-hearing children may or may not have a richer language development than totally deaf children, but they will still experience some sense of isolation in situations where they cannot be full participants in conversation. This is especially true in group interactions or in areas where there are prominent background noises. This book is not directed primarily to hard-of-hearing children, but we should mention that all too often parents and educators have the unrealistic expectation that hard-of-hearing children can be fully integrated into the hearing world. Closer examination of the social and psychological situation of these children and adults reveals that they are acutely sensitive to their differences and to the lack of understanding of their difficulties by well-meaning hearing people.[6] This is especially true when they are placed in situations that require that they conform to classroom and social activities geared to those who have no hearing loss. Gross gaps in knowledge have been demonstrated in those areas where the lack of hearing has resulted in the failure to understand classroom instruction. The written language of congenitally hard-of-hearing children will sometimes reveal what they have missed.

As the deaf child matures and he recognizes that oral conversation and reading are the chief modes of communication and learning, his sense of isolation increases. He must still, however, resort to action and gesture to communicate his wishes. If the parent demands that the child speak, it intensifies this feeling of isolation.[7]

The parents' feelings crystallizing around their concept of hearing loss as a bodily injury represent a distinctly different psychological orientation from that of the deaf child. Ordinarily they do not reconcile this difference. The psychological differences between growing up deaf and growing up hearing are not superficial but profound. However, the degree of isolation is an area now open for correction. Methods of communication are available permitting the exchange of information between the parent and child. These methods will significantly reduce the sense of isolation between them.

Isolation from others is perhaps one of man's greatest concerns. No one can exist in a vacuum. Our capacity to communicate meaningfully with others is inextricably tied to our capacities for survival. A diminished capacity renders one compromised; a nonexistent capacity to communicate renders one impotent.

The grief, anger, guilt, and helplessness stimulated by the discovery of the child's deafness seldom disappear completely in any parent. Although most achieve various partial resolutions of these painful emotions, it has been the authors' clinical experiences that the mildest empathic probing of parents' feelings will inevitably reactivate an intense but transient grief. This has been observed in parents of young children as well as in parents of deaf offspring now in their forties.

The Resolution of Feelings Toward a Child's Deafness

As explained previously, the child's deafness has superficial meanings for the parents as well as deep psychological implications. Some problems such as educational methods can be resolved by conscious decisions. However, the deep psychological implications are not easily resolved, especially those that prevail each time a new frustration taxes the parents' capacity to cope.

The disabled child directly challenges his parents' capacity to cope with novel parental experiences. His mother and father cannot easily look to other parents of deaf children for advice or guidance under ordinary circumstances. The mode of reaction for each of these parents is too individual and the incapacities of their child too variant. In addition, educational programs either do little to get parents together to share common feelings and experiences or else they actively try to prevent parents of young deaf children from interacting with parents of older deaf children. [8] This shields the parents of the young child from the obvious speech difficulties of the older deaf child and the regrets and bitterness of the other parents. Furthermore, deaf parents of deaf children and deaf adults, from whom a hearing parent of a deaf child could learn so much, are often excluded from parent groups because their views are contrary to prevailing educational philosophies.

When confronted with their child's deafness, the parents begin a process, which if successful will allow them to abandon the hope of having a perfect and normal child. The original concept of the infant's future must be replaced with more realistic notions of the limits imposed by the disability. Only with a realistic appraisal of the deaf child's capacities is it possible for the parents to help him achieve the maximum within his limitations.

The parents are rare who realize initially that their child's accomplishments will be significantly altered and limited by deafness. These parents waste no time in readjusting their notions of their child's capacities. They quickly recognize that achievements in speech and lipreading will be quite limited and that the traditional educational process for the deaf child will be slow, laborious, and inefficient. They shift from an unrealistic concept of the child's future to a more practical one. Unfortunately, such an ideal situation rarely occurs. Such realizations usually come too late and limit remedial efforts.

Most often, parents adopt positions with the child that are based on unrealistic assessments of his capacities because of their inability to relinquish fantasies of normality and perfection. Many things can lure them away from their unwanted psychological burden. Perhaps the greatest temptation comes from the deaf child's visible similarities to his hearing peers, except for deaf children with obvious physical handicaps. Among these similarities are vocal utterances similar to the sounds of young hearing children up to the age of eighteen months, early play patterns that closely duplicate those of hearing children, and normal achievement of certain growth milestones such as creeping, walking, and running.

When considered in its own right, the promise of possible communication with the deaf child is a powerful and sustaining force. A sense of completeness and maternal success grows in the mother as she communicates with her child. As for the child, the absence of full communication with his mother leads to alterations in his development; it can limit his capacity to develop feelings of closeness to his mother and subsequently to the other members of his supporting culture. The child's limitations in communication with his mother prevent her from feeling that he has successfully attained his growth milestone.

If the professional community holds out an unrealistic promise that meaningful communication will eventually occur between the parent and child, the parents are inclined to overlook their immediate inability to communicate effectively with their child.

They will endure their child's meager achievements if the eventual "pie in the sky" is normal speech and communication. That is why parents of five-year-old deaf children can allow themselves to speak with pride of their child's vocabulary, which may be less than five words. The intense psychological need for a "normal" child leads the parents to interpret this failure to develop communication not as the failure it is but as a promise of things to come. With the acquisition of the first word or the establishment of rudimentary gestural communication, there will be temporary relief of their feelings. As the child matures, however, and needs for complex communication skills increase, differences between the deaf child and his hearing peers become more noticeable, and the parents' anxieties will be reactivated.

This does not mean that there is no communication. A limited communication accounts in part for parents' ability to tolerate this seemingly intolerable state. Through exchanges of feelings and inventive gestures, the parents and the child can communicate to some extent in some areas of basic need; and love and anger are easily communicated without words.

As the years go by, most parents gradually accept the limits of communication imposed by deafness. They sink into a state of bitter resignation. Eventually, some are able to assume a more realistic attitude, but by then irreversible psychological and educational damage has occurred. The many potentialities the child had die unrealized, and parent and child are denied fulfillments that could have been theirs. A prime goal of this book is to prevent this unnecessary tragedy.

Perhaps the most difficult psychological burden to handle is the anger that the frustrations of deafness make an everyday part of life with a deaf child. It has been our observation that this anger is seldom if ever completely relieved.[9] Each new frustration in understanding and meeting the child's needs serves as a new stimulus. This observation and its ramifications are central in understanding the role of the combined method of communication. A successful communicative vehicle for exchanging critical information as well as tender, or angry, feelings can provide much gratification to parents. Improved communication reduces frustration, which in turn reduces anger.

As noted earlier, anger when not recognized will find outlets, nonetheless. It can interfere with the parents' objectivity in caring for the child and punctuate the relationship with angry outbursts. Kind words that conceal angry feelings do not necessarily go unnoticed by the deaf child. He must rely more heavily on nonverbal signs of communication such as facial displays of emotion. He will watch feelings parade across his parents' faces to obtain crucial information in ascertaining intent and good will.

If the parents fail to resolve their feelings of grief, anger, guilt, and helplessness, they will be forced to remain arrested in the earliest stages of their psychological reactions to the child's deafness. This is the stage discussed earlier wherein the primitive psychological processes of denial and rationalization form the chief mode of handling the psychic pain caused by the child's deafness. Through such mechanisms, parents may find temporary relief but no solution to the more basic and enduring problems of developing communication. The deaf child is placed in the position of having to drag his parents along, demanding at each new stage a new adaptation from them, which they feel ill-equipped to handle. It is our belief that the parents' early reactions related to the discovery of deafness and their resolution of these feelings toward the child influence all future decisions.

The Role of the Professional Community

In reflecting on their experiences during the deaf child's infancy, many parents have voiced resentment toward members of the professional community who held back or misinformed them of the major issues about the deaf child's future adaptation. Parents may direct their angry feelings toward physicians who stalled them off, teachers who promised more than oralism could deliver, or audiologists who may have failed to deliver a clear message about the extent of the child's hearing loss.

It has been reported by some families that pediatricians minimized their concerns, delaying definitive diagnosis to unspecified future times. Occasionally, such pediatric clichés as "it's a phase" or "he will outgrow it," are heard. These kinds of suggestions and remarks are unfortunate and costly mistakes. They lead parents to procrastinate further over something that has already given them many months of anxiety. Recollections of such experiences often form the core for many of the angry indictments later hurled at the medical profession.

Unfortunately most physicians, including otolaryngologists, are unaware of the most basic issue in childhood deafness: how the condition interferes with the normal progression of the child's language and psychosocial development. Traditionally, they assume that once responsibility is handed over to this or that educational establishment, the future of the child is assured. Physicians at large must be apprised of the real issues to avoid being unwittingly drawn into this kind of delusion.

It must be recognized by these professionals that parents are vulnerable to anything stimulating their unhappy feelings during the early stage of discovery. Whether hearing aid dealer or physician, the first professional to whom the parents speak about their child is being asked for much more than a diagnosis. The parents' grief and anxiety is at its height. Their uncritical vulnerability is related to factors not within their conscious awareness. Up to the time the diagnosis of deafness is made, parents have been unable to rid themselves of the belief that the child is deaf, despite their repeated acts of denial and rationalization. There are practically no professionals who are prepared or who will attempt to deal with the parents' primary need: to discuss, ventilate and understand their feelings toward their deaf child. It is not uncommon for the busy physician or audiologist to feel that his responsibility has been fulfilled once he has established the diagnosis of irreversible deafness. This is only the beginning of the time of parents' greatest need.

Most professionals struggle with their own feelings over having to tell parents something that will hurt and upset them. Thus, they are often inclined to assuage the parents' anguish by offering sympathy. Such offerings lead to temporary relief only and tend to delay more effective procedures. Such offerings do not remove the feelings or help parents to develop more realistic coping techniques.

What conclusions are to be drawn from the above discussion? When parents have been informed that their child is deaf, the feelings of grief following definite diagnosis must be acknowledged. The mobilization of constructive mental health resources is sufficient acknowledgment. Referral to centers providing comprehensive services is essential. It is the responsibility of the mental health professional to provide direct services to the parents, as well as to enlighten other concerned professionals about the relevant psychological phenomena of this period. Then they in turn will be more able to handle these issues with more sensitivity and sophistication. What actually happens in individual cases after deafness is diagnosed depends upon whom the parent gets for counseling and the age of the child when the advice is given.

It has been almost universally recognized that the early identification and habilitation of the deaf child brings the best results. The principal problem lies in the nature of the habilitation recommended. To date, the most common advice is the use of early amplification and instruction in oral speech and lip reading. The controversy and fallacy of these as the sole techniques will be discussed in the chapters: "Hearing Testing and Related Issues"; "Social, Educational, and Language Development," and "Oralism versus the Combined System."

As we have demonstrated, the manner in which the parents interact with the child and act on his behalf is determined by many different factors. As a consequence, the appropriate intervention is necessarily a team intervention. Such a team should ideally consist of competent professionals in education, audiology, psychology, social work, psychiatry, neurology, and whatever other medical or paramedical services are required such as ophthalmology or physical medicine.

It is a universal observation of those who have constructed programs for special groups of young disabled children that unless the parents' emotional needs are adequately dealt with, the programs themselves have limited benefit for the children. One of the great appeals of oralism has been its simplistic appeal to needy parents that this method will directly alter what is most obviously defective about the child: his inability to develop conventional language and speech. Equipping the parents as soon as possible with a technique that purports to do this narrows their anxiety and temporarily allays their grief. But this does not relieve the primary problem of how they are to deal with their enduring grief.

In this chapter, we have discussed the unfolding of childhood deafness and its effect upon the family. The goal is to achieve a flexible parent-child relationship impossible without adequate communication. If this goal is achieved, parents can fulfill their responsibility of providing an effective link between the child and the world beyond the home.

There is a close correlation between the parents' early reactions to the discovery of the deafness and their future handling of the child. Those reactions which mire the family in bitterness and resentment can be prevented by early enlightened professional intervention. Successful family adaptations to childhood deafness are rare today because of narrow habilitation efforts. As a consequence, deaf children become progressively more isolated from their families and from the hearing community as well. This occurs despite the *common and misleading* dictum: "The deaf child must learn to get along in the hearing world."

Chapter 3

The Primary Causes of Deafness

Suspicion that a child may be born deaf may arise during pregnancy if inherited deafness or maternal rubella (German measles) are involved. Severe neonatal jaundice due to the incompatibility between the blood of the mother and her infant may produce damaging conditions causing hearing loss before or just after birth. In such cases physicians may apprise parents of the possibility of deafness. Hearing loss may also be due to a severe infection in later childhood that affects the brain or its covering membranes. If the onset is prior to the time the child has started speaking in sentences—about eighteen months to two years—the loss may not be immediately recognized. If it occurs after this age when the child has begun to communicate verbally, the deafness will be apparent immediately.

Disease Processes Causing Deafness Prior to Birth

There are two major causes of congenital deafness: genetic deafness and rubella! Deafness in the offspring is anticipated most often when one or both parents are deaf, presumably on a genetic basis. Deaf adults often do not know the cause of their own deafness. Members of the current community of deaf adults, at the time of this writing, were born at a time when there was less focus on birth defects. Establishing the cause of deafness at that time was a much more random process. It is likely that many cases formerly thought to be inherited were due rather to *subclinical* maternal rubella.[2]

If there are profoundly deaf individuals in the lineage of either of the parents of a deaf child, the child's deafness is most likely to have a hereditary cause. Nondeaf parents who have deaf grandparents or other close relatives may have some concern that their child will be deaf; if most of their relatives have normal hearing, their concern need not be great.

Heredity

Genetic factors have been the leading cause of deafness throughout this century except during certain epidemic periods of rubella. Generally, 50 to 60 percent of all deafness is attributed to genetic factors.[3]

It is often surprising to professionals in deaf habilitation and rehabilitation work—and to parents—to discover that 90 percent of genetic deafness is carried by a recessive gene. This fact is especially surprising in cases where there may be no known deafness in the immediate family. The lottery of genetics is such that, although this recessive gene for deafness is present in approximately one out of ten persons, only six children per ten thousand are deafened genetically.[4] The recessive gene in one parent has to be matched by one in the other parent if a recessive trait is to appear.

Children deafened through hereditary causes are less likely to have other defects than children deaf from nongenetic causes. As a group, the genetically deaf do better in school.[5] There is also evidence to suggest that, as a group, they may have slightly higher intelligence test scores than deaf children generally have.[6]

Paradoxically, parents are generally loath to accept the fact that their child's deafness is of genetic origin. They react to such a diagnosis as if it stigmatizes them. In view of the common-ness of recessive gene carriers and the excellent achievement record of genetically deaf children, this attitude, though understandable, is certainly unnecessary.

Where genetic deafness is suspected or established, the family should take two important steps. First, competent genetic counseling should be sought in order that all family members can be made fully aware of the probabilities for deafness in future offspring. Second, regular and complete ophthalmological examinations should be sought because, of the fifty-seven known forms of genetic deafness, there are ten that involve *both* hearing loss and visual problems.[7]

Rubella

Between 1963 and 1965, a rubella epidemic raged across the United States.[8] It resulted in the birth of more handicapped children than did the thalidomide disaster. Educational programs for deaf children are at present hopelessly overwhelmed by the number of children from this epidemic. Whereas rubella usually causes about 10 percent of children's deafness, those preschools serving youngsters born during the 1963-1965 period report a 40 to 80 percent prevalence of postrubella cases of deafness. This means that over one-half of all deaf children under the age of six were deafened by rubella.

Rubella is an incipient disease. A mother will be aware of the illness if she has developed a rash, swollen lymph nodes in her neck, and low grade fever, but often the disease does not come to actual clinical definition. A study was made of mothers of infants who had rubella virus cultured from the infant's urine at birth. The study revealed that 50 percent of these mothers were unaware that they had been infected during gestation.[10] When the rash occurs, it is typically evanescent, and when the mother appears for examination by her physician two or three days later, it may have already disappeared.

Although rubella virus usually causes only a mild illness, it can seriously affect a developing fetus. Deafness is most frequent, but visual problems (cataracts and/or retinal damage), lowered intelligence, or heart defects can also occur.[11] Studies at Johns Hopkins Hospital indicate that 85 to 90 percent of postrubella infants suffer significant physical damage during gestation.[12]

The period of greatest danger to the fetus is the first three months of pregnancy, but damage can occur if the mother is infected even within a few weeks prior to conception, or as late as the eighth or ninth month.[13] Rarely is there significant damage to infants infected after birth.

The rubella virus is not necessarily eliminated from the infant's tissues after birth. It has been cultured from infants as old as nine months. It can remain within various cells of the body and continue to cause cellular damage for, as yet, an undetermined period of time.[14]

Vaccines have been developed and are being distributed that give promise of eventually eliminating rubella as a major cause of deafness.[15] Primary concern remains as to the effectiveness of these vaccines to control epidemics without undesirable effects to the recipients.

Regular physical and audiological examinations are important for postrubella youngsters. Since the probability of other problems such as poor vision, heart trouble, and neurological damage are high, these possibilities must be thoroughly investigated by pediatricians, ophthalmologists, and other appropriate specialists.[16] Sometimes, the parent must assume responsibility for seeking specialized examinations for the child because the family doctor may not always detect subtle visual or neurological difficulties.

Diseases of the Perinatal Period Causing Deafness

There are two prominent causes of deafness related to this period. These are prematurity and blood type incompatibility between the mother and the child (especially where the fetus is Rh positive and the mother Rh negative).[17] As a consequence of blood type incompatibility, the infant becomes jaundiced during the first twenty-four hours of his life. If the jaundice is severe and an exchange transfusion is not performed soon enough, products caused by blood cell destruction are deposited in various areas of the brain.[18] Infants with hearing loss or cerebral palsy are the common sequels.[19]

One would not expect parents to anticipate deafness in a premature infant or one having blood-type incompatibility. Some pediatricians may advise parents of the possibility, especially in the case of a jaundiced infant. Most physicians and other professionals do not wish to alarm parents unduly. Physicians, however, should consider these infants as high-risk cases and should follow them accordingly.[20]

Premature Birth

It has recently been discovered that four times more deaf children than nondeaf children are born prematurely.[21] Approximately 17 percent of deaf youth of school age were born prematurely.[22] While the condition itself is rarely a direct cause of hearing loss, the association between prematurity and deafness deserves consideration. This is particularly true when the child is born prematurely and no other cause of deafness can be isolated. Conditions such as lack of oxygen and cerebral hemorrhage, which can damage the nervous system, are more common among prematures* than among full-term infants and can cause deafness.

When a child is known to have been born prematurely, he should be regarded as a high risk for hearing loss. If deafness is diagnosed, it must be remembered that thorough physical examinations should be made to check for other problems, especially those involving vision, central nervous system, and the heart. The probability of these kinds of difficulties is heightened in children known to be both deaf and premature.

Complications of Rh Factor

Certain genetic combinations of blood types in parents result in blood incompatibilities between mother and child during pregnancy. One of these occurs when Rh negative mothers have Rh positive fetuses. The mother's antibodies will cross the placenta and enter the bloodstream of the fetus destroying his red blood cells and leading to a severely jaundiced newborn baby.[23] When this occurs, death may result at or soon after birth. Of those who survive, a large proportion are deaf.[24] Many of these may also have cerebral palsy or problems in language development in addition to those problems due to deafness alone.[25]

Advances in medical science may soon eliminate Rh incompatibil. as a significant cause of deafness.[26] Postnatal and in utero blood transfusions are preventing some of the effects of this incompatibility. In addition, a special gamma globulin has been developed, which when administered to an Rh negative mother after the birth of her first Rh positive child will eliminate the destructive anti-Rh positive antibodies from her blood. This means that her second Rh positive child stands the same chance of being affected as the first child; for without the elimination of the destructive antibodies he would be in more immediate danger of damage.

Diseases Resulting in Deafness During Later
Childhood

Destructive processes during diseases such as meningitis and encephalitis can cause deafness.[28] There may be damage to parts of the brain that are crucial to language learning.[29] The child thus affected has special problems in subsequent language development. After the age of two, it has been observed that most children are able to develop greater language capacity at a progressive rate from that point forward. It is not a linear development, however, during the age period between two and four years (see chapter five).

A child freely communicating with his parents until the onset of meningitis or encephalitis, who is then deprived of this communication, has difficult adjustment problems. The fear of having almost lost his life

---

*A premature infant is defined by the World Health Organization as an infant weighing five pounds eight ounces or less at birth.

may also accompany the loss of speech because the disease processes leading to hearing loss also threatened his life. Such may have been the parents' concern too. The near loss of a child can leave parents feeling they must now treat the child with special interest.

Meningitis

Approximately 10 percent of deafness in children is caused by meningitis: an inflammation of the meninges, the protective coverings of the brain and spinal cord.[30] The disease deafens an estimated three to five percent of the children who contract it.[31] The chance that deafness will develop depends in part upon the organism causing the meningitis.[32] Several organisms can infect the meninges.

A major clinical problem of meningitis is that clinical symptoms, such as headache, stiff neck, or fever cannot be readily diagnosed in infants and young children. Infants cannot specify the location of their discomfort to the doctor or their parents and can only react to the situation by irritability or tears. Hence, the disease is often not diagnosed immediately. Sometimes it is only when evidence becomes clearer—a fever above 100 degrees, a seizure, or a coma—that the child is taken to a doctor or hospitalized where the laboratory tests required for definitive diagnosis are made. Often an unavoidable delay in instituting therapy may lead to deafness. The fact that premature and very young infants are especially susceptible to meningitis compounds this problem.

The development of antibiotics has greatly improved the survival rate for most victims of the disease. But, introduction of antibiotics into clinical medicine has also changed the characteristics of postmeningitic children.[33] Previously very young children, especially premature infants and infants less than one month of age, died from the disease. Now they survive in significant numbers and frequently have residual effects of sufficient magnitude to interfere with normal adaptation. Examples of clinically detectable effects on the nervous systems are learning disorders, muscle weaknesses, paralyses, and deafness.[34]

As a result, most of today's postmeningitic deaf children lost their hearing before they were old enough to have learned language through hearing it. Thus, they lack vocabulary, syntax and speaking skills. Prior to the extensive availability of antibiotics, postmeningitic children had usually learned some language because they were older when they contracted the disease. Because so many of today's postmeningitic children had the disease when very young, and because the disease frequently causes additional neurological damage, our educational methods for these children must change correspondingly.

Encephalitis

The viral organisms that cause such diseases as mumps and the two-week measles may subsequently invade the brain, causing encephalitis.[35]

One result may be deafness. When this occurs, there are often other disabilities such as learning difficulties and behavior disorders.

Misconceptions About Causes of Deafness

It is not uncommon for the lay public to consider "brain fever," a blow on the head, or a high fever that "burned up the nerve," as the reason for a child's deafness. It appears logical to connect these events to the deafness, since nearly all parents can recall times when their child received a hard blow on the head or had a high fever. This reasoning seems valid when the deafness is discovered at two or three years of age and when there is no other known cause.

Fever alone does not cause hearing loss, nor is a blow to the head likely to do so unless it is severe enough to fracture the bones of the skull that protect the auditory mechanisms. These mechanisms are well protected by the bones of the skull and are located on both sides of the head. Fractures damaging hearing in both ears simultaneously would be a rare possibility. Unless such damage or a specific disease such as meningitis is identified, it must be assumed that "brain fever," "burned up nerves," or "falling from the cradle" are unlikely explanations. At best these are inexact reasons for a child's deafness.

It is helpful for parents to know the cause of their child's hearing loss. Although the loss itself is unalterable, the knowledge will generally reduce the parents' tendency to blame themselves. Furthermore, establishing the etiology may prevent the birth of additional deaf children and be of value in treating and understanding the child. It is especially important for the deaf child to have frequent, thorough medical checkups by a pediatrician and otologist. Neurologists and ophthalmologists should also be consulted to provide care for defects of the nervous system or visual defects that may coexist with the deafness.

Chapter 4

The Testing of Hearing and Related Issues

The people who test the hearing of a child having a suspected hearing loss can be, and often are, the pivotal people in the child's life. It is upon their findings that predictions and plans are made for the child's future education. Any information given on the child's hearing impairment must be translated into the question, "Is there sufficient hearing available for the child to acquire conventional language and speech?"

Conventional language and speech means language and speech learned by those who can perceive speech sounds normally, as contrasted with the distorted speech sounds heard by those with defects of the inner ear mechanism or auditory nerve. Profoundly deaf individuals are those who do not receive speech sounds clearly enough through their hearing to develop language, even though they may be aware of loud or random noises.

Often when the auditory mechanism is damaged, the result is not just a diminished capacity to hear sounds or simply a reduction in the amount of sound impulse transmitted to the brain. A damaged auditory mechanism will also transmit distorted or poor quality impulses. Therefore, the ability of the brain to interpret sound information is severely compromised because of the altered nature of the sound signals. Hearing capacity is really a function of the individual's ability to discriminate and understand the sounds that reach him. "Blasting in" just any sound with high-powered hearing aids may be of no help.

Given these limitations, one can generally say that the child with a profound hearing loss does not have the equipment to learn language and speech through hearing. Continuous efforts to expose the child to sound are an exercise in futility.

Following Up Initial Suspicions of Hearing Loss

It is important that all observations suggestive of hearing loss be brought promptly to the attention of the family physician or pediatrician, otologist or audiologist. The parents' observations regarding the child's hearing have great validity. The sensitive physician or audiologist will take great care to question the parents thoroughly about their suspicions. Once the parents feel that something is definitely wrong, they must not be content with statements that delay getting the information they need. Clichés such as "he will soon grow out of it" do not suffice.

When observation of the child continues to suggest the possibility of a hearing loss despite professional reassurance to the contrary, parents should not discount what their eyes, their ears, and their intellects tell them. In the last analysis, it is the parents and not the professionals who have the responsibility for the child's destiny.

As explained in chapter two, some of the parents, fortunate in getting correct diagnosis and guidance early, find these facts unacceptable and cannot appropriately alter their expectations. They "pound the pavements" from physicians to audiologists, to educators or hearing-aid dealers seeking a magical cure or a diagnosis of normal hearing. Their fruitless search only postpones acceptance of the truth.

Determining Hearing Loss: Formal and Informal Methods

There are two groups of methods by which hearing loss is determined: the audiologist's tests and informal tests. In the former, it is important that the audiologist testing the child has an extensive background for evaluating children's hearing. The methods used are quite different from those used with adults, and special skills and experience are required. Good pediatric audiologists are able to conduct a relevant interview with the parents to get information about the child's hearing functions at home, where language activities occur the most spontaneously. It is very important that they understand the sensitive emotional climate in families of children with hearing losses and the real limits of the method and materials which they employ to evaluate hearing loss. These qualifications are the ideal but are not always obtainable.

With children under three, or with older children whose cooperation cannot be obtained, audiologists may have to rely on additional test procedures. These are similar to the kinds of observations parents often make, but attempts are made to control the pitch and loudness of the sounds. The audiologist may try to determine how loud the sound of a rattle, bell, or toy horn must be before the infant responds. The sound level at which the child reacts is carefully noted. Because many deaf children are very alert visually, parents as well as examiners can be fooled. The visually alert infant may be turning his head in response to something he sees rather than to something he hears. Many audiologists insist on testing a child several times to determine if the responses to sound are consistent from test to test. [1]

The second group of methods consists of informal tests by people other than audiologists. These are not tests in the sense that they are published, formally circulated, or routinely utilized by professionals. They are procedures based on chance observations of the child's hearing behavior by parents or other concerned adults. For example, a mother may notice that her young child is not awakened by the noises she makes when she walks into his darkened bedroom; yet, he wakes up when the bedroom light is turned on. Or, the child may not turn around when the parent walks unseen into the room and calls him. After developing an initial suspicion based on such incidents as these, many parents will try other home tests, such as dropping pots or making loud noises behind the child's back. The audiologist will later refine such makeshift techniques into a more controlled test situation.

Pediatric audiologists find that it is often impossible with currently available formal testing procedures to develop a firm diagnosis regarding the degree of hearing loss until the child is about two to two-and-one-half years of age.* During this age period, it becomes possible to gradually condition the child to respond to sounds. This means that the child learns to perform an act such as dropping a block when he first perceives a novel test sound. Novel sounds such as the pure tones [tt] produced by the audiometer are used along with typical environmental sounds such as music or speech. These sounds are played into a room or through earphones at different levels of loudness.[2]

How Hearing Loss is Classified

The following scheme outlines the functional hearing which can be expected at various levels of loss as measured in decibel units.[ttt] These categories are generalizations based on pure tone averages.[tttt] There is a great deal of variability from child to child. Therefore, such a classification scheme serves only as a gross outline.

Normal: 10 to 25 decibels (dB). No significant difficulty with faint speech.

Slight: 25 to 40 decibel loss. May pass unnoticed, or the child may have difficulty hearing faint or distant speech. If there is difficulty in school situations, the extent of the difficulty will be dependent upon how near to 40 dB the loss is, the distance from the sound source, and the quality of the sound.

Mild to moderate: 40 to 55 decibel loss. Generally understands conversational speech when the distance is limited (in the range of three to five feet). If the child is tired or inattentive, the difficulty in hearing will be greater. Factors such as distance, noise extraneous to the conversation, and poor articulation or soft speech often affect how much practical difficulty the child will have.

Moderately severe: 55 to 70 decibel loss. Sounds must be loud and distance small for conversation to be heard. Child will have considerable difficulty unless conversation is directed exclusively to him.

Severe: 70 to 90 decibel loss. Even shouted conversation most likely will not be heard. Speech cannot be learned by conventional means with this degree of loss.

Profound loss: over 90 decibels. Although occasional loud sounds are heard, the child perceives vibrations rather than complete sound patterns.

Parents frequently ask audiologists to classify their child's hearing

---

*In discussing the age range for valid testing, some difference of opinion is expressed among audiologists. Some believe that a truly accurate test cannot be obtained until the child is four years old.

ttPure tones—mechanically or electronically produced sounds of a certain frequency or pitch: usually, 250 H_z (cycles per second), 500 H_z, 1000 H_z and 2000 H_z. The 250 H_z tone corresponds to middle C on the piano. 500 H_z is one octave higher, etc. They differ from the sounds produced on musical instruments, however, because there is no resonance, that is, there is no simultaneous production of related sounds. It is resonance that imparts the rich quality to each tone of a musical instrument. The tones of the human voice are not pure either, but consist of broad and complicated sound patterns.

tttThis table is based on the standards established by the International Organization for Standardization in 1964. (H. Davis, "Guide for the Classification and Evaluation of Hearing Handicap.")

ttttPure tone average is based on the amount of hearing for the frequencies 500, 1000 and 2000 H_z, the *speech frequency range.*

loss in decibel units or percentages.[3] Although the decibel has been employed to classify losses, it has limited usefulness in conveying an accurate picture of the child's disability. The unit is actually a way of measuring the physical energy of sound, not loudness per se. The A.M.A. has developed a formula for computing hearing loss as a percentage. This is of little use today, because of its complexity and its relative meaninglessness in telling the patient or his family about the functional consequences of the hearing loss. It was developed primarily for use in determining compensation for industrial hearing loss. More useful information for the parents is how loud the sound must be before the child can actually hear it. Loudness is the psychological counterpart of the decibel and more accurately reflects the child's actual hearing situation.

How Impaired Hearing Is Aided

The role of amplification (hearing aids) in helping people hear better is a complex subject.[4] There are certain limitations to be noted. As stated previously, raising the intensity of sound delivered to a damaged inner ear does not necessarily imply that the child will be able to understand what he hears.[5]

As for what a hearing aid can do, it is important for parents to realize the difference between realistic expectations and understandable wishes that the aid will "cure" deafness.[6] Hearing aids are frequently seen as a panacea and parents, lulled into a false sense of optimism, come to believe that the solution to their child's deafness has been found.

For the profoundly deaf, amplification generally serves only to create sensitivity (awareness), but contrary to popular belief the understanding of distinct sound patterns and speech is impossible.[7] There is no evidence to substantiate the notion that sound awareness contributes to the development of a speaking vocabulary or linguistic competence. In no instance will sound awareness insure that a deaf child will have normal speech.

The implications of these facts are of great importance and should be thoroughly understood by parents. The use of a hearing aid should not be justification for delaying the implementation of other educational activities to help the child to develop language capacity (see chapters five and six).

Residual Hearing

Residual hearing is a catchall phrase referring to the hearing available after damage to the auditory mechanism has already occurred.[8] It can refer to useless sensitivity to low-pitched sounds, or to functionally useful remnants of hearing in the higher pitched ranges. Unless the amount and extent of residual hearing is defined, this information, given to parents, can create an unrealistic fantasy that the child will develop normal speech and language—that he will no longer be deaf.

Speech consists of a relatively narrow range of pitches, mostly between 300 and 4000 cycles per second. The value of residual hearing depends, in part, upon a combination of loudness and pitch—the loudness required before the sound can be heard by the child and the pitch ranges (cycles per second) the child can hear. Therefore, the potential for learning speech through residual hearing may be nonexistent or it may be excellent. Interpretations concerning the significance of residual hearing in relation to speech and language should be given conservatively. Unfortunately, they are generally too optimistic.

Audiologists have encountered persons who have normal hearing only at the higher frequency ranges—2000 or 4000 cycles per second. With this preservation of hearing, these rare individuals have been able to develop normal language and speech. This is apparently because they can perceive consonant sounds accurately. Consonants carry the information of speech, and are heard as high frequency sounds. Unfortunately most deaf and hard of hearing children have the least hearing in these high frequency ranges.

Early Infant Screening

During infant screening procedures, testers expose the infant to a variety of sound stimuli in the newborn nursery or well-baby clinic. They frequently use sirenlike sounds of a certain pitch. By noting infant responses such as eye blinks, crying, stilling responses, the Moro reflex (see page 40), or eye-widening, the audiologist may gain some notion about whether an infant is responding in an expected fashion.[9] He may also employ other testing devices such as wooden clackers, rattles, and horns; but these instruments are difficult to calibrate to the level of sound intensity necessary for eliciting a response. Currently, infant screening finds its greatest usefulness with high-risk infants in cases where maternal rubella is known to have occurred, where there is a family history of deafness, or where severe jaundice was a postpartum complication. When properly employed and interpreted, such screening can alert the pediatrician to possible hearing or developmental problems such as infantile autism or mental retardation. The procedure should serve this purpose only, and under no circumstances can a diagnosis of hearing loss be made.

As valuable as we hope early infant screening is, its diagnostic validity in long term follow-up is not presently known. Controlled studies covering the results of the screening procedures have been made. These studies revealed that the number of children suspected of having a hearing loss who did not actually have a loss was large enough so that hearing aids are generally not recommended before the child is one year old.[10] There is evidence suggesting that early amplification prescribed on the basis of infant audiograms may destroy remaining hearing by overstimulating the auditory mechanism.[11] Most audiologists who advise putting hearing aids on high-risk infants below the age of one year do so only under strict supervision.[12] Results published in the popular press of the miraculous benefits of early amplification are most controversial and generally not well accepted by the profession.

Cortical Audiometry

In recent years, researchers and clinicians have developed a complex electronic technique to study brain wave changes caused by sound impulses which are recorded by the electroencephalogram (EEG).[13] This technique is called *EEG* or *cortical audiometry*. Our purpose in discussing this technique is not to offer information as to its scientific merits but rather to inform parents and others about reasonable expectations from this procedure.

Parents of any group of disabled children are understandably prone to transfer hopes for cure or dramatic amelioration of their child's handicap to new scientific developments. All too often, this transfer is given impetus by unrealistic and uncritical reports of writers for the mass media. Electronic equipment with a mystique born of its seeming incomprehensibility especially garners groups of hopefuls around it. Something as complex as cortical audiometry easily arouses false expectations.

The technique is carried out in a standard testing environment devoid of extraneous noises and other stimuli which can also cause particular electroencephalographic changes similar to the ones being measured. In addition, a sophisticated expense piece of equipment is used — the *average response computer*. The overall procedure, in addition to being expensive, requires considerable technical skill. More importantly, the results must be analyzed and interpreted by the human operator.

Concerning the current status of this technique, it may be said that (1) its use is limited to well-financed research projects manned by experienced and well-trained personnel; (2) even with financing and staffing, the results are at times equivocal; (3) it offers no hope in the immediate future for providing a sure method to measure hearing on a scale that will fully serve the needs of the young deaf and hard-of-hearing population; (4) recent publications on this topic are not enthusiastic on the use of the procedure as a threshold determining technique* with all children; (5) at best, it is another technique which may assist in the diagnosis of a hearing problem and not the panacea, which the popular press would lead parents to believe it to be.

The Successes and Exceptions

There are young children who are thought to have significant hearing losses but who eventually develop greater vocabulary and language ability than anticipated. These are usually children who originally were misdiagnosed. They are often hard-of-hearing or have progressive or adventitious‡‡ losses.[15] Some are children in whom the capacity for developing language is delayed for reasons not well understood or children with

---

*Thresholds are determined by noting the decibel level at which hearing responses first occur when pure tones are introduced in the sound field. This is different from assessing speech discrimination ability; the ability to perceive and interpret speech accurately.

‡‡Adventitious hearing loss is a term used for hearing losses that occur from injury or disease at some time after birth. Deaf adults who have been adventitiously deafened generally have better speech and language.

emotional disturbances interfering with the development of language. When professionals include them as members of the severely and profoundly deaf community and then point to their communication skills as realistic goals for deaf children, they promote false hopes in parents.[16] It has been our observation that some oral education programs use such children as examples of successes to justify a continuation of the oral educators' avowed course.

Within every category of human function, there are those exceptional individuals with a larger share of certain aptitudes than others. For example, piano lessons most often produce piano players, not virtuosi. So it is with speech lessons and deaf people. But, the hope for such exceptional success constitutes a cruel trap for parents. The hope that their child will be a "virtuoso" can keep them from taking the necessary steps to insure their child's full development within the confines of his disability. Hope that a deaf child is an exception may be stimulated by professionals to help parents ward off uncomfortable psychological reactions that follow the discovery of their child's disability.

Some may regard our view as fatalistic, which it definitely is not. It is rather a plea to allow the child to be what he can be. Parents hurt their child by allowing themselves to be drawn into states of wishful thinking by professionals or fellow parents of deaf children.[17]

The Use and Abuse of Aphasia and Autism

There are two groups of exceptional children whose hearing is intact but who show little or no responsiveness to sound. Among these are aphasic children and autistic children. Aphasia refers to a disability either in the child's capacity to correctly interpret incoming sounds or in his capacity to correctly produce words or sentences. The latter is not due to a defect in his sound production mechanisms (vocal cords, et cetera) or a damaged hearing mechanism but rather to his brain's inability to program word or sentence production.

Many children who have failed to respond to traditional lipreading and speech techniques have been called aphasic.[18] In a hearing person this diagnosis is established after an assessment of language capacity. Since deaf children do not develop language normally, making a diagnosis by observing inadequate development of speech and speechreading is tenuous. As with any nebulous medical condition with inadequately established criteria, these conditions become catchalls.[19] Deaf children, so labeled, are often placed into groups of multiple-handicapped children, whereupon the standards for achievement are immediately lowered. They are categorized as depreciated children.[20] They attract fewer professionals to work with them. Many classes for these children amount to "holding operations" otherwise known as baby-sitting. Children may remain in these classes well into their teens.

A few words about autism must suffice. This is an uncommon psychiatric disease of children. One of its major characteristics is the child's inability to relate to others in a human way; he relates best to inanimate objects. The autistic child treats other human beings mechanically, as if they were also inanimate. His behavior is highly idiosyncratic. He may show an affinity for things that twirl or will spend much time twirling himself. He can remain absorbed in seemingly insignificant acts such as pouring water from one container to another for long periods of time. He will remain quiet until such activities are interrupted. Then there may be violent outbursts of anger. The use of speech is delayed or he may remain mute. His response to sound is often unusual, giving the impression of deafness even when he is stimulated by very loud sounds.

There are some personality traits of deaf children that are suggestive of autistic behavior. Especially, of course, is the nonresponsivity to sound and the tendency to impulsive outbursts when their routines are interrupted. Because the deaf child has limited access to environmental information, he demands a high degree of order and predictability. This helps him maintain his stability despite limited external cues. The diagnosis of autism is not one to be made by educators or audiologists. This requires the service of child psychiatrists and psychologists and social workers.

It has been our experience that most parents of children with suspected hearing loss pass through a period of emotional turmoil and confusion over establishing appropriate goals for their child. A parent adequately apprised of the merits and pitfalls in current methodologies is spared considerable anguish. A sophisticated and sensitive audiologist can put parents on the right course from the outset by delivering realistic information.[20] It is incumbent upon physicians to refer suspecting parents to appropriate sources for testing. Parents must be helped to understand the intricacies of hearing loss. And, following that, claims for remediation by hearing aids must be given conservatively.

From time to time, parents of deaf children with other disabilities will become aware of new developments. We are all conditioned to look and hope for them especially when definitive help for difficult diagnostic problems is remote. Something so complex as cortical audiometry could easily be regarded in this expectant way. If it is held out as promise for establishing absolute diagnosis of hearing loss it can become a false hope. Everyone hopes that the perfect hearing test will soon become available. But, the point we wish to emphasize most is that it *can* be used by parents to delay further the implementation of effective remedial measures — measures that will ensure an adequate development of the child's language competence.

We have discussed briefly the successes and the exceptions. The exceptions can be deceptions if knowledge of them is accepted uncritically by parents. Many factors bear on the outcome of the deaf child's educational, social, and emotional development. Some of these elaborated elsewhere in the book are the family's capacity to accept the deafness, the child's basic intellectual endowment, the emotional health of the child, the adequacy of the school system, or the possibility of concurrent brain damage. Everyone hopes that the child they are working with will be the exception. It does not mean, however, that one communicates differently with one child than another. All children with inadequate language exposure and development are shortchanged.

Chapter 5

Social, Educational, and Language Development

Language development, social growth, and the educational process are closely interdependent in the deaf child. The outcome of his educational and social adaptation is directly related to his language competence not his speech performance (see p. 47). Specific information regarding these outcomes will be given in chapter 7. What follows is a synthesis of the information from several groups of investigators that demonstrates the relevance each has for a comprehensive understanding of the deaf child's development. For example, a careful reading of Jean Piaget's demonstrations of evolving cognitive structures is most important in establishing age-related learning ability.

Basic to our thesis is the conviction that learning is a natural process that cannot be forced. Piaget and other early and contemporary developmentalists of the nonbehaviorist school have established the dependence of learning on inner drives and capacities. These investigators have shown the necessity for the child's active involvement in the learning process. The child's cognitive work is in the construction and modification of internal models which establish object permanence and spatial, temporal, and casual relationships which are the consequence of the child's active participation in the learning process.

It would be valuable to outline the Piagetian scheme of learning to the teaching needs of deaf children. This would result in a more specific tailoring of teaching materials and methodologies to the cognitive capacities of the children. That, however, exceeds the goals of this book.

Our discussion of the development of affective (emotional) and social structures in the early years of life derives from psychoanalytically oriented investigators including Rene Spitz, Anna Freud, Erik Erikson, and Harry Stack Sullivan.[1] The emphasis on the biological ordering of language development is given comprehensive definition by Eric Lenneberg. A discussion of the evolution and form of the biological matrices underlying the development of language are found in *The Biological Foundations of Language* and other works.[2] A careful study of this volume is a must for professionals who work with deaf children.*

---

*Also see: *The Capacity for Language Aquisition,* pp. 11-28, David McNeill in Research on Behavioral Aspects of Deafness, New Orleans, La., May, 1965. U.S. Dept. H.E.W., V.R.A., Wash., D.C. 20201. *Developmental Psycholinguistics,* David McNeill, pp. 15-84 in The Genesis of Language - A Psycholinguistic Approach. Editors: Frank Smith and George A. Miller. The Massachusetts Institute of Technology Press, Cambridge, Mass. *Communication, Psycholinguistics, and Deafness,* pp. 4-15. Proceedings of the Teacher Institute, Maryland School for the Deaf, October 17, 1969.

The Deaf Child's First Year

Distinctive characteristics develop early in the unfolding relationship between the deaf infant and his mother which distinguish this relationship from the conventional situation between a mother and her nondeaf infant. One reason for these differences is that communication patterns between mother and deaf infant are not established in the conventional way. How soon this difference that develops from the communication loss becomes apparent is not known precisely. Of crucial importance is how the difference creates a sense of distance between the mother and the infant which, in turn, causes later alterations in the personality development of the deaf individual.

For background purposes, we will briefly discuss the development in the first year of the biological and psychosocial matrix from which later communication patterns evolve. A review of some aspects of normal development provides insight into possible long-term effects of distortions in the early mother-and-deaf-child relationship.

The First Three Months

During this time, social communication between the mother and infant does not occur. The infant is relatively oblivious to his surroundings and sleeps most of the time. Biological need is indicated to the social environment simply by his crying, fretting, or restlessness.

The infant is not born with the expectation that particular individuals will respond to his distress. Anyone can satisfy his simple demands. His limited responses to outside influences are essentially reflexive and instinctual. Inborn responses to sound which are present at birth, include blinking, rapid horizontal movements of the eyes (nystagmus) and head. No higher order of thinking intervenes in this reflexive behavior. The infant is dominated by the stimuli arising from within his body or from his environment. If a loud, sharp noise occurs or he is dropped gently on his back, his arms will fan out in front of him like ratchets and he will cry (the Moro reflex). If shouted at, he responds to the loudness, sharpness, or suddenness of the sound but obviously not the meaning of the words.

Initially, the infant's vocalizations have no specific meaning, no semantic content. Referred to as *global tone language,*[3] they are not sound patterns learned from the environment because nobody in the environment cries that way except other newborns. These vocalizations show the inheritance of a vocal mechanism with the function of signaling that the infant is physically uncomfortable (wet, hungry, etc.). By the fifth week of life, the global tone language is differentiated into sounds that are instinctual expressions of various emotional states such as pleasure, discomfort, hunger, pain, or anger.

Because the early sounds are often not specific, the mother must find the source of the child's discomfort. She checks the room temperature and notes how well the child is protected; she checks if diapers need changing. Several hours have elapsed since the infant was last fed and her breasts are filled. This mother-child reciprocity—the child's instinctive communication of need, and the mother's attempt to respond appropriately—is necessary in setting the stage for the later months when formal social communication evolves.

The infant during the first three months does not have a psychological relationship specific to his mother. This develops when he is capable of remembering sufficient features that will unmistakably mark her in his mind. During this period almost any individual can make the infant comfortable, but there must be adequate physical contact between infant and a nurturing adult. If not, infants can become listless and weak. They will cry more. If deprivation of contact is severe and prolonged, grimacing and odd gestures may appear. These behaviors are reversible provided adequate mothering is reinstituted within the first three months.

Initially, then, in the mother-child transaction, the infant is a "demander," but a passive recipient. Activities centering around his feeding and other biological processes are the focal interpersonal experiences. For the mother, an infant restfully feeding in her arms affirms her capacity to mother successfully, and her womanliness.

The changes which occur in the quality of this early relationship reflect the growth of the infant. For example, by the beginning of the second month, the infant can see a person approaching. If he is crying in hunger when approached, he will become quiet then open his mouth and make sucking movements. From the outset, the mother's face is associated with pleasurable experiences. When the infant feeds, he does not gaze at the bottle or the breasts, but at the mother's face.

Beginning at the end of the second month (and up to six months), the infant shows more specific response to the face of another. When he sees the forehead, eyes, and nose of a nodding head, he smiles. Cooing often follows. It is the first truly social sound. Although crying is his first vocalization, it is not a precursor of speech nor necessarily a step in its development. Crying undergoes some change in the quality of sound during childhood and then persists unchanged throughout life.[4]

When the ability to smile and coo appears in response to a human face, rudimentary interpersonal communication is established. Because these responses are genetically determined, they are present in deaf children as well as hearing children.

A mother experiences a deep sense of maternal success when her infant smiles. She feels responsible for the pleasure that his smile signifies. Now the infant becomes active in the mother-child unit because his smile causes changes in her feelings. Since these feelings are often pleasurable, the mother looks and yearns for signals that indicate satisfaction in the child. Thus, by the age of three months, the infant, by biological endowment, can attract, sustain, and encourage the mother's involvement.

Three Months to Six Months

During this period the infant attends to many more aspects of his environment than those of the feeding and holding experience. For example, he learns to discriminate his bottle from other things. He can perceive depth.[5] Beyond the initial smiling response to a straight-on presentation of the face, he can now perceive its three dimensional qualities and its size and color characteristics.

Concurrently, with the appearance of depth perception in the visual field, the ability to localize sound develops. For example, the four-month-old infant turns his head and searches for speakers. At five months, he can specifically identify his unseen mother by her voice. To illustrate, if the mother enters the infant's sound field and talks but remains unseen while the infant is crying in hunger, his cries will be stilled.

Six Months to One Year

Contrary to general opinion, most parents of a deaf child develop a definite conviction that their child is deaf by the time he is six months of age. Often, this is not articulated. But the sense that the child does not hear is there. It is the authors' unsubstantiated opinion that suspicions about hearing disability develop earlier, even in mothers who have no reason to suspect that their child will be deaf.*

If the deaf child is not her first child, the sensitive mother has an inner set of developmental expectations concerning the infant's growth, of which she may or may not be consciously aware. These stem from her observing the growth of the first child. The deaf child showing variance from these expectations will alert her to a possible difference. Even if the deaf child is the first, one could speculate that through evolutionary processes, mothers are "programmed" to expect vocal or behavioral responses to their vocalizations; they expect complementarity in their communications with the child. When the child does not respond as the mother is primed to expect, she develops a sense of incompleteness and dissatisfaction. It may be experienced as an ineffable gnawing feeling, which she is not necessarily conscious of during the early months of her infant's life. Perhaps the mother's feeling is no more specific than an uneasiness about her child. She may say, "things are just not right."

By about six months, the form of the vocalizations have innately shifted from cooing to babbling by the introduction of consonantal sounds "ma, mu, da, di" in both hearing and deaf infants.[6] In the deaf infant, these consonantal sounds are likely to persist in nearly unmodified form until much later. With the hard of hearing, auditory training is successful in linking them into groups of sounds that approximate word sounds.

Modifications in these early sound patterns begins near the end of the first year in the hearing child. It is chiefly the frequency of certain babbling sounds that seems to distinguish the hearing child's vocalization from that of the deaf child. There seems to be an agreement that sound production during the deaf child's first year is quantitatively less than that of the hearing child.[7]

There is a difference of opinion on whether or not there are phonetic

---

*The psychological factors which retard "discovery" were discussed in chapter 2.

differences between deaf and hearing children. Lenneberg has observed that laughter and sounds of contentment in nonhearing children seem identical with those of hearing infants.[8] Others have reported that the crying pattern of deaf children is melodically distorted with more screeching and less emotional differentiation.[9]

Although the infant's sound productions are not reliable indicators of hearing loss, infant responses to sound at six months are. For example, by sixteen weeks of age, the child can control his head movements when he hears a sound, as contrasted to earlier behavior when random head movements were the reaction to sound. The mother is gratified to see this; it strengthens her impression that she is a meaningful person to the infant. In the deaf child, this reaction does not take place, and its failure to occur has great psychological significance.

At six months the infant can move his entire body in response to sound. By then the mother of a deaf child has developed a suspicion of his deafness based on the accumulation of clues. She is then likely to try some homemade tests to which she does not get predictable responses (see chapter 4).

At six months the infant achieves other developmental milestones which allow the mother and infant to engage each other more directly. He can sit up and watch the mother during meals which allows face to face communication. This allows the mother to scrutinize the child's face more carefully for evidence that he is or is not responding to her voice.

At eight months, when intonational voice patterns are beginning to form in the hearing child, the deaf infant does not show such variation. (The intonational patterns of older deaf children, although not phonically smooth, can communicate emotion effectively.) The deaf child shows no discriminations; he will make the same nonspeech sound regardless of what he desires to communicate. Obviously, since the deaf infant has not heard speech, he cannot be expected to exhibit sound alterations analogous to those in the speech of his culture.

At nine months, there is true imitation of speech in the hearing child.[10] He repeats sounds of his own speech repertory and some that he hears in the environment. In contrast, at one year, babbling in the deaf child stops for the most part.[11] This is a dramatic cutoff and signals the shift of speech from a vocalization process that is primarily dependent upon internal biological programming to one related to the available sound milieu in its continuing development. When "ma—ma" is being developed as a standard vocabulary word in the hearing infant, the deaf infant clearly begins the lag in his development. Under the present educational system, he not only never catches up but actually falls further behind.

Twelve to Eighteen Months

Although it would appear that a child's language growth can be measured one word at a time over the next six months, there is evidence that these words are used in a more discrete fashion. For example, the one-year-old hearing child may use "da-da" to refer to any caretaking person, male or female. Later, but before eighteen months, the child may say "da-da" if his father suddenly stands up at the dinner table. Whereas at one year of age, "da-da" means, "I am in the presence of a caretaking person," later it can mean, "My father has just gotten up from the table."[13]

During this period the young hearing child is also developing his capacity to produce basic sound patterns in the speech of his culture. Often, we are amused by the young hearing toddler's jargon which sounds like something we should recognize, but we can rarely identify distinct words. It is like the music but not the words of speech. In addition to "da-da," we may hear many other words frequently used at home such as "milk," "doggie," or a sibling's name. Thus, from twelve to eighteen months, the child increases his vocabulary but applies terms in a broad way and begins to reproduce the rhythms and sounds of the language in his environment. The deaf child cannot do this.

Interpersonal Relationships and Character Development

Some personality differences between the deaf and hearing child are subtle, some are obvious. The differences in the deaf child's capacity to relate meaningfully to people are so subtle as to prevent us from characterizing them. His need to express frustration physically, often by temper tantrums, is an obvious difference. Our main interest, however, is in answering the question: How does the altered communication between the mother and her deaf child change the nature of this child's future relationships with her and with other persons who have meaning for the child?

Work with deaf teenagers and adults has opened a pathway for insight into this question.[14] Limitations in social development, difficulty in communication, and unfamiliar sounds combine to produce in hearing people, even parents, a sense of alienation from the deaf child or adult. The essence of this alienation derives from the deaf child's inability to respond to the hearing person in a complementary manner; i.e., he cannot give the expected verbal or social response. Thus, there is lack of complementarity. The hearing adult senses less distance and isolation in the deaf child whose family has used manual communication with him from an early age. The available opportunities for communication allow the child to explore and develop more fully his social relationships.

Communication in the early months is characterized by the exchange of feelings. The paradigm for this is the effect of the infant's instinctual smile on the mother: she is gratified by the smile and drawn more fully into a relationship with the infant. With the development of language skills, verbal communication plays an increasingly important role in social activity. Instead of expressing feelings through a smile or other actions, more and more feelings are channeled into and expressed through language. Distaste may be expressed verbally, not just by throwing food on the floor. There are exceptions. In certain adult situations, such as love-making and war, feelings are not channeled into language. In the former, the regression from the verbal level of communication is appropriate and gratifying; in the latter, the regression is destructive to the self and society and represents a failure of that society to channel its aggressive energies appropriately.

Another effect of deafness according to some authors is the characterological rigidity attributed to deaf adults. We have looked at the behavior and the circumstances of the deaf child's life for ideas on the origins of this rigidity and have observed that because deaf children are restricted to visual cues, they will enter fewer group settings. They must "hang back" and analyze a social situation without benefit of explanation by adults or peers. The child can make his wishes known by demonstration only, which is a very limited form of expression.

But there are other causes of this rigidity as well. In an average home with its confusing array of "do's and don'ts," the parents' teaching techniques with the deaf child are usually restricted to demonstration or punishment. A one-year-old hearing child can learn the implications of a small vocabulary of imperative statements delivered in a commanding tone, such as, "sit down," "no," and "hot," whereas the disciplining adult must often strike the young deaf child in a punitive manner to achieve an effective equivalent to the restrictive tone he would otherwise use with a hearing child.

During the toilet training period, when the child's social responsibility achieves greater definition, a parent may resort to spanking for failure rather than gentle admonishment or explanation. Such overreactions cause perplexity that can instill a feeling of danger in the child which he may experience whenever he approaches new situations. Social experiments can soon lose their pleasurable aspects and become fraught with anxiety. This situation, true for all children, is especially true for a deaf child.

Many parents have expressed their helplessness in developing flexible methods for establishing reasonable social behavior. A reaction against the need to teach or set limits through punishment may lead them later to overindulgence of the child. The parents may allow the deaf child greater latitude at home than is desirable for his character development.* Those things a hearing sibling would be punished for, the deaf child may be "let off" from. Many parents mistakenly feel that such attitudes contribute to the child's growth. Too severe disciplinary methods or too much leniency are found frequently in families of deaf children.

Interpersonal development outside the home is often equally impeded in deaf children. Earlier, when the participation of speech is not a necessary part of play, deaf children play easily with hearing children. Soon, however, deafness tends to limit the range of activities in which they can engage and feel gratified. For a more specific illustration, consider the

---

*The term, character, as used in this book is consistent with psychiatric terminology. It refers to the composite of the psychologic systems and structures which mediate the individual's behavior. It does not refer to the moral judgments implicit in the lay use of the term.

game "playing house." Much of this game consists of talking about and acting out parental roles or roles of other significant adults through imitation. Playing house partly represents an effort by children to understand and define the relationships of people close to them. The complexity of the play patterns will depend on the age and maturity of the child and upon data gathered in previous experiences in or out of the family. The learning of parental roles through such verbalization and play with other children is not ordinarily available to the deaf child; he must depend upon his own "figuring out" capacities and not upon explanation to learn about role relationships.

In sum, transactions between the deaf child and his parents tend to be characterized by extremes of punishment or overindulgence rather than moderation and verbal explanation when possible. The deaf child's access to information on adult roles is limited and so too are his opportunities to learn from certain kinds of experimental play with hearing children. Characterological rigidity is often the consequence of all these influences.

The Educational Environment

When the deaf child enters school, he should have the opportunity for progressive expansion of his social and communication potential. Some growth does occur, but there are philosophies and methodologies currently present in the general field of education that have been applied to deaf education and which prevent further expansion of the latter. Beyond the fundamental educational and social losses that result from regarding oralism as the comprehensive approach, there are other damaging misconceptions. For example, one basic question all educators must ask, but often do not, is "How much learning is due to what the child is told, versus, how much learning occurs as a consequence of letting the child explore and express himself."* Related to this are the maxims found in many teaching methodologies that "the child must be made to learn," or "the child must be taught how to think." They have numerous corollaries and they are often spoken of as if fact. Though many will disavow belief in them, analysis of actual practices, attitudes, and methods demonstrates their prevalence and influence.

Such maxims violate basic principles of cognitive development. The nature of cognitive development depends on innate patterns which establish the modes and limits of the growth. The emotional and cultural environment in which the individual grows and his health (physical intactness) establish the cognitive content.

Whether or not information is integrated by the individual derives from the innate drive to learn, an already developed capacity, and not from being "made to learn."

Psychological development as contrasted to physical growth is less

---

*It has been demonstrated that communications in classes for deaf children are predominantly those originating from the teacher. Deaf children are thus actually prevented from expressing themselves freely as an essential factor in intellectual exploration and development. (Craig and Collins, "Analysis of Communicative Interaction in Classes for Deaf Children.")

easily understood, in part because of its intangibility. Under ordinary circumstances, significant aspects of it are neither noted nor recorded. Documenting physical growth, or establishing theories about it, is far less forbidding. We can observe that our twelve-year-old nephew, living in New York, has grown five inches taller since we last saw him. Chances are, however, we will not bother to observe any changed competence in his handling of the grammatical complexities of his language.

"Learning" through drills has traditionally filled endless hours of elementary school time. The introduction of the new math was, in part, an effort to reduce some of this time expenditure. Each child is allowed to discover mathematical relationships as if the relationships had never been known before but the discovery is predicated on already-developed cognitive capacities to handle quantitative spatial and temporal relationships. Language growth develops in an analogous way. The child develops an increasing ability to work with the complexities of the language of his culture. Despite the solid evidence for the overriding importance of the innate linguistic capacities, most teachers and many parents of deaf children believe that by endlessly repeating words (Pestalozzian* pedagogy gone wild) the child will become a proficient user of the English language.[16] Why is this dogma accepted by so many?

It is evident that the number of areas of learning one can study and grasp is limited by factors such as time, preference, ability, and experience. In school we had to accept that "the teacher's word is law." Because most of us have been processed through a similar educational system, we have accepted the teacher's role as primary, her techniques as fact. In order for the child to pass smoothly through his schooling, he and his parents must learn the ground rules established by the school and the individual teachers, regardless of their effectiveness in facilitating learning.

Thus, when the teacher of the deaf child specifies that for the child to develop linguistic competence he must constantly practice certain words, most have traditionally accepted it because a teacher said it. Furthermore, we often fail to discriminate between speech and language, especially in the field of deafness. We have assumed that being able to say (or parrot) a word implies language competence.

Many of the words spoken in the presence of deaf children are words that are easy to speechread. They do not necessarily contribute to language development at the appropriate level of meaning or grammar. An example is the often heard phrase, "You got an *ow*," rather than the appropriate phrase, "Did you hurt yourself?" The lip configuration of "ow" can be speechread but that of "hurt" cannot. There are thousands of such examples, and they dominate the communication between the deaf child, his parents, and his teachers. Instructions given to teachers and parents to speak facing the child, encouraging him to watch the face, give little or no consideration to whether or not the child has achieved sufficiently mature linguistic competence to utilize the observed lip movements.

---

*Johann Pestalozzi, Swiss Educational reformer—1746-1827.

Our brief discussion on education has come to focus on language development. This is a logical necessity because it is the core problem of the deaf child's education. To understand these issues more fully, we must consider language development as an independent issue.

An Overview of the Development of Linguistic Ability

The phrase "deaf and dumb" is unfortunately well-known. Earlier in history, the inability to hear was associated with an inability to make sounds. The erroneous assumption which followed was that it was possible to demonstrate defects in the brain which prevented deaf people from speaking. The manual sign for deafness earlier carried the suggestion of inability to speak. To sign "deaf" one pointed with his index finger, first to his ear and then to his mouth: "Ears shut, mouth shut." Now it has been appropriately modified. One points first to the ear and then brings hands together parallel to the ground with the palms down. This combined sign means "ears closed."

Much of the habilitative effort on behalf of the deaf has been to correct the "unspeaking" aspect of deafness. Contemporary professionals want to demonstrate that the deaf are not dumb. They want to avoid that depreciatory implication by teaching the deaf to speak! But, the deaf child's acquisition of articulation skills does not necessarily mean that he has developed language capacity. To repeat an extreme case for purposes of illustration, a trained parrot can speak, but he does not have human linguistic ability. The parrot can repeat words or phrases, but he can not define the words he articulates.

Although they do not account for language development, certain conditions must exist if linguistic ability is to develop in the normal way. First, there must be intact hearing. Second, the developing child must be where he can hear typical samples of his culture's language used in their appropriate contexts by mature speakers. (This is the area on which the oralists have predominantly focused their attention.) Third, there must be no damage to the central nervous system that prevents fully elaborated linguistic competence. Fourth, the emotional stability of the child and his family must be such that his capacity for language acquisition can be maximized. These four are necessary conditions in order for normal development to occur. Each of them assumes special significance in the deaf child; for none can be taken for granted in the absence of conventional language development.*

Many educators of deaf children have fallen prey to simplistic associationist theories of learning in which language development is thought to be a mere association between word and action or thing.[18] This naive

---

*The special limitations of the deaf child in coping with these conditions were discussed in chapter 4, will be discussed further in chapter 6, and are elaborated throughout this book. Impaired hearing is covered in chapter 4; problems with hearing speech samples are covered in chapter 6 and throughout the book; damage to the central nervous system and emotional problems are considered later in this chapter.

notion is the heart of oralism. Anyone who has struggled to educate a deaf child or has tried to account for the failures can readily see the appeal in this notion. Complexities born of variations in hearing function and the mysteries of *minimal brain damage* leave the professional in a theoretical melee. In discussing language development, we will consider individually three component parts of language: the sound system, the grammar, and the semantics.

The Sound System

The sound system comprises recurrent patterns of vocalizing, i.e., words, phrases, intonations, stresses, etc. These vocalization patterns are not absolutely constant in that they are variously modified through dialect or accent; or they may serve for emphasis, to pose a question, to convey warmth or humor. These modifications give additional information to the listener.

Sound patterns can undergo considerable modification but still remain intelligible. For example, a two-year-old child's rendition of words or phrases can be at considerable phonetic variance from that of a mature speaker but can still be understood by a mature listener. Sometimes it is necessary to hear speech within its relevant context to know the intended meeting. To illustrate, "ahgosiu" might be unintelligible until the child is seen looking at his feet, at which point "all gone shoe" would become evident.

Sound patterns undergo further modification when placed into sentences and paragraphs. The total intent of the communication as embodied in the construction of the sentence will lead to still further modifications of the sound patterns. If one wishes to convey firm conviction, the words will have a different emphasis than if one wishes to be humorous.

Eric Lenneberg has demonstrated that the development of all components in language are dependent upon growth changes of the central nervous system.[19] Naturally, if one has never heard formal spoken language, he could not speak intelligibly. His speech would consist of primitive noises heavily laden with feeling tones and would be imitative (onomatopoeic) in character.

Those who have heard the utterances of profoundly deaf young children are familiar with the natural sounds they make. Although these sounds are recurrent, they cannot be regarded as real spoken language rudiments. That is because in the normal evolution of speech ability, the child does not first learn the component sounds of words then to be combined later into conventional words. Such an assumption is naturalistic and is based on hearing the child babble before speaking recognizable words.

The foregoing is one of many misconceptions that comprise oralism's pedagogy. Oralism depends upon the early innate development of babbled sounds as usable rudiments for oral skills. But after the babbling period, phonetic development in the normal child proceeds not to combinations of these rudimentary sounds, but to the exploration and development of *broad sound patterns*, the jargon referred to earlier that seems to resemble adult sound patterns.[20] From the *broad sound patterns,* there are further differentiations of the sounds as they come to more closely approximate and later duplicate standard phonetic patterns of the culture's language.

A second misconception with far-reaching consequences is that the normal child practices his speech before he develops the "correct" sound. Lenneberg clearly disputes this and states flatly that in the hearing child, "practice is not a prerequisite for speech development."[21] The child's innate maturational timetable allows for continual differentiation of phonetic output, so he is progressively more capable of mature renditions of speech. Thus, the countless hours spent in practicing speech by the deaf child does not duplicate the process of speech development in the hearing child. Further, these drills are usually started two to four years after speech development begins in the hearing child; and, there is no evidence to substantiate claims that early oral training produces more fluent speakers.

The occasional sounds which resemble conventional speech sounds tantalize the parent of the young deaf child. "Ma — ma" or "um — um" or "muh — muh — muh" sounds of the infant babbling period, may seem to offer the promise of greater speech performance than the hearing loss would indicate. It is these sounds which make the two misconceptions elaborated above more attractive — the misconceptions that mature speech develops from independent sound combinations, and that the normal child practices his speech to "correct" sound.

Grammar

The second relevant component of language is the system by which words are arranged into forms and sequences to convey additional concepts over and above the dictionary meaning of the words. We refer to this system as the grammar of a language. Grammar traditionally consists of morphology and syntax. The former term refers to the modifications (inflections) on the basic words to signify such things as plurality (s, es) or past tense (ed), for example. Morphological refinement is a later development in language maturation; it is generally completed by age eight. The latter term, syntax, refers to the arrangement of words in a sentence according to the way they function in the structure of the sentence.

The study of a person's syntax enables one to plot in a steplike manner this particular evolving mental capacity — the increasingly complex manner by which his thoughts are expressed through language. This is contrasted to traditional approaches to child development in which certain features of speech or motor capacity have been described at their various stages without establishing the cognitive connectedness between the stages.

Of chief interest is the time when a child shows the capacity to combine words, even into two or three-word combinations, for he has begun the process of formal language development. Single words as global concepts — all men are daddy — come to be combined with other concepts, expanding the possibilities of linguistic expression. Thus, the "simple" addition of the adjective "big" to the noun "house" demonstrates a capacity to differentiate the concept "house" into varieties of houses. Through complex mental operations, phrases and sentences convey information of increasing sublety and magnitude about objects and indicate the developing ability to categorize (group and organize) and concatenate (join into linear combination).

There is an orderly development to syntactical capacity. The child is said to proceed systematically and largely automatically through a series of increasingly complex grammars.[22] Compared to adult form, these early grammars are "ungrammatical." But it has been shown that "me do" is not ungrammatical for a two year old. Were we to demand that a child use an alternate form such as "I want to put on my own pants," we would have little success in convincing him to change his grammatical form. He might answer, "pants," and continue to use his current grammatical form.

Syntactical capacity has been shown to develop through sequences universal to all human languages. The early simple constructions of the child such as "a train," "my house," or "all gone milk" are found in analogous forms in the various languages of all children.[24] Gradually, the grammatical forms shift to those determined by the culture.

There is a "pregrammar," but no formal grammar before age eighteen months. The child moves toward and away from familiar people and things. He establishes predictability in interpersonal relationships. He discovers that some things have permanency, others are temporary. Some things are his, or some belong to others. All this that lies behind his expressive language remains largely uncommunicated. Associated feelings, however, can be communicated. Thus, the child has a limited ability to tie linguistic utterances to all conceptual aspects of a given experience, which he has perceived. His full capacity to do this comes later when the child can objectify his experiences and can express their connotative richness.

Gradually, the capacity for abstract thought and its expression through language becomes possible. Language achieves independence from concrete experience so that things and people can be considered in their absence. When the young child begins to link his words, he is demonstrating that his capacity to consider meaningful relationships between people and things has increased. Although such abilities develop on schedule in the deaf child, he cannot express his understanding of these relationships until sometime after the age of five. The feedback that naturally accrues from the expression is almost nonexistent.

Traditionally, educators assume that the deaf child will develop the adult grammatical forms without proceeding through primitive grammars initially. The reason for this assumption is that formerly linguists did not study developmental grammar. Most of their effort went to make word counts or define phonetic refinements. Now, with a rich and fascinating literature available on developmental grammar there is little reason for continuing to use methods based on outdated information.

One of these methods still popular in schools for the deaf is the

Fitzgerald Key, or Barry Slate Method. This is a series of printed examples of mature grammatical structures used with deaf children six years of age and older. From the use of this key, the child is expected to discover grammatical relationships that were four or more years developing in the average hearing child. This places an intellectual burden far too challenging for the mind of any young child.

Semantics

The third component of language in the three-part language system is the semantic. Investigations in this area attempt to discover how the organism uses language to organize experience and thought.[25] Thus, the child exposed to the language of his culture learns that people, things, and actions can be referred to by specific words or word groupings. But learning the associated words does not nearly constitute an understanding of the meaning of the thing. The common misconception is that meaning is embedded in the word. More accurately, the word is embedded in the meaning.

The child's cognitive capacity assesses the significance of people, things, and actions. Much of what he discovers remains unspoken but comes to comprise his body of semantic knowledge. When he is ready to communicate about a given topic, he examines the input for meaning and draws upon his body of knowledge for appropriate response. Knowledge is not like an encyclopedic collection. It is an operational understanding of ideas in their original and subsequent context and their participation with other ideas.

It does not appear that the semantic component can be neatly separated from the syntactic, for it is by mentally "moving around" concepts into various linguistic positions that meaning is developed and communicated. When semantics or syntax are thought of in static form, the implication is that an individual is forever welded to thinking according to strict formal definitions of words and general grammatical usage. Noam Chomsky's example that there is a very slight chance of one ever finding any one sentence of a daily newspaper repeated at any time in the future does not support this implication.[22]

When teachers attempt to wed the child's linguistic output to formal definitions and constructions, the child is being forced away from man's natural bent, which is perpetual creativity in the use of language. Sign language, no doubt, persists despite efforts to stop it because it readily conforms to natural linguistic expression. For example, two deaf boys have met for the first time. Using the appropriate manual communication, they first ask each other to demonstrate a sign for their names. One boy is named Aaron; his hair is strikingly blond. He holds his fist in the "A" position and places it near his hair. The second boy is named William. William wears glasses. He holds his hand in the "W" position near his glasses. Each boy is thus "named" by association with an outstanding individual feature.

Exchanging names does not end their project of coming to understand each other. They observe countless traits and actions of each other. Some will be commented on. In order to do so, they rely on their analytical cognitive capacities. With associated linguistic abilities, they explore meaning and structure it into ordered sequences which they communicate. Each time they do this, it is a totally dynamic linguistic exercise.

To enable deaf people to communicate with the same linguistic freedom of hearing people, they must be freed from the inhibitions and prohibitions created by static notions of language usage. Existing methods of teaching by vocabulary words and formal grammar has forced communication into static patterns.

The use of a simultaneous manual-oral system allows linguistic ability to be continually expressed, not limited by a rigid communication system. When a deaf person does not know a word for something he has observed, he can pantomime it. This does not mean that he is arrested at an early stage of development when children are learning by imitation among other methods. It means only that he is seeking a way to readily convey that a particular person, action, or thing has meaning to him and in calling another person's attention to it, he is inviting a mutual exploration of those ideas. As various properties of this new thing are communicated about in context, further relevant properties can be elaborated. It is through such processes that semantic growth occurs.

Language creativity functioning in a deaf child is demonstrated in the following description by the mother of Abraham, a deaf child, using a simultaneous system.

> Last summer, our son's summer-program teacher came to our house for a sign-language class. She is deaf; her fiance, also deaf, was to teach the lesson. Abraham exhibited the same delight, disappointment, competition, and curiosity as our hearing children have when they learn that here was his teacher's boyfriend to whom she was to be married. We found him a delightful, bright, and mischievous guy. Abraham sized-up this competitor for his teacher's affection, and sensed an important part of the young man's personality, calling out to him in sign-language, "You're a little devil!"

Abraham was thus able to exercise the language function known as *metaphoric extension* when he called the teacher's boyfriend "a little devil." Parents with deaf children taught by the oral method seldom, if ever, can point to examples of such creative use of language or the humorous naming that is also demonstrated.

The "Critical Stage Hypothesis"

The "critical stage hypothesis" as applied to language development assumes that for normal language to develop there must be a combination of intact hearing, undamaged linguistic capacity, and proper language stimulation during the first three to six years of life. Basic to this hypothesis is the belief that once these early years are passed, one cannot expect an individual to achieve mature linguistic ability. But, there does not now exist a dependable body of theory relating this hypothesis to deaf children. Oralism ignores the critical stage theory, for embedded in its pedagogy is the notion that the early noncommunicating years can be made up for by vigorous oral training, which concentrates on speech performance. Concern for meaning is ignored. Analysis of typical fragments written by adult deaf people demonstrates that this is not the case. Here is a typical fragment of the written language of one deaf woman who attended a leading private school.

> "I feel sorry for you have hard life your three children also your wife. I know children bothers parents so much so the children wants to do something, but I sees children do that. Parents are not patients, but some parents are very patient children. I know is hard to teach children to learn things. Do you and your wife feel hard life or easy life with children?"

An interpretation of the above fragment follows:

> I feel sorry for you. You have a hard life with a wife and three children to care for. I know that children bother [worry] parents so much. The children want to do things the parents do not want them to do. Many parents do not have patience with their children. I know it is hard to teach things to children. Do you and your wife feel that your children have made your life an easy or a difficult one?

Bonnie Litowitz, as a graduate student in psycholinguistics, analyzed the grammar in a large collection of this woman's letters containing samples such as the above. In her preliminary analysis, she found that the woman developed a grammar which differed from that of hearing peers in the quality and complexity of formulating rules according to syntax. Correlation between rule use and lateness of rule acquisition in a normal grammar was revealed which supports the assumption that there are optimal periods of language development. When this period is passed because deaf people must "stretch out" their language-acquiring time — due to slow and frustrating methods — some difficult rules may never be acquired. Complex sentence subleties and interrelations, such as the use of conjunctions, are among those areas found to be inaccessible to the deaf woman whose language she studied. For example, the woman could not render a normal sentence such as, "The nurse gave me some medicine for my pain." Rather she produced, "I took few medicine for pain so the nurse gave me." She used two concrete simple sentences and incorrectly connected them by the conjunction "so" instead of uniting and condensing the sentence.

We are aware of one study in which arrests in grammatical development were somewhat altered in adulthood by a careful use of manual communication in a language rehabilitation program.[27] This is another area of considerable importance in providing intelligent rehabilitation services for deaf people.

Brain Damage

Today, the issue of brain damage concurrent with deafness is most relevant because of the large numbers of children deafened by rubella.[28] Rubella and the other major diseases resulting in deafness are also prime causes of brain damage.[29] Children with handicaps in addition to deafness are often labeled "multiple-handicapped." In many schools for the deaf. such groups are comprised of children varying from those with genuine mental retardation to those who have failed the oral method, or rather to those whom the oral method failed. The naive assumption is made that they have an additional problem — "aphasia, brain damage, or retardation" because they have not learned orally.[30] Both of the authors have encountered numerous adolescents and adults who were diagnosed as "multiple-handicapped" on such a basis and were discovered later to have adequate intellectual endowment. In fact, many school programs classify up to 40 percent of their deaf students as multiple handicapped, when the real problem is the inflexibility born of an orally-based program.

There are, unfortunately, too many misguided souls in the deaf education establishment who believe that deaf children are in actuality retarded and must be regarded that way educationally. Some superficially sophisticated studies have been done which purport to demonstrate an actual difference in brain function.[31] This fatalistic and poorly substantiated view holds that this is an irrevocable effect of deafness that will not yield to proper communicative techniques. Thus, regretfully, outdated concepts about lacks in the deaf person's thinking capacities have been elevated to the level of stated or implied educational philosophies. Many students graduating from college still believe and propagate these misconceptions.

As soon as statements such as the above are made, however, it becomes necessary to issue a caution. It is often possible through medical examinations and psychological and educational testing to establish the presence of concurrent learning disabilities, which interfere with the educational process. When such assessments are made, parents and teachers should not be drawn into a situation wherein they feel that if the child would only work harder, he could overcome his handicap. Rather, they should attempt to provide the specific teaching techniques which would enable the child to circumvent the concomitant handicap.

Emotional Disturbance

Emotional factors have a direct influence on the learning behavior of the child. The development of the initial emotional climate in the deaf child's family discussed in chapter 2 merits reemphasizing. When initial reactions to having a deaf child are not adequately resolved in the family, they continue to exert a retarding influence on the deaf child's adaptation. Unresolved emotional factors continue to manifest themselves and have the effect of keeping the child pathologically bound to the family and to nonadaptive coping patterns. The child's delayed emotional development prevents him from moving on schedule into appropriate adolescent and adult roles. The older the child gets, the greater is the family's frustration.

Techniques for evaluating emotional disturbances in the deaf child have not been well formalized at the present time. There are very few child psychiatrists with experience in this area and even fewer who devote a significant amount of their professional time in this field. There are several obvious reasons for this. Perhaps the most salient reason is that there are only eleven hundred fully trained child psychiatrists in the United States. A second reason is that most problems of deaf children are traditionally considered to be in the province of education and aural rehabilitation. A final reason, of greatest interest here, is that without extensive experience in working with deaf children, it is nearly impossible for the average child psychiatrist to fully understand the behavioral problems of the deaf child.

In general, psychiatrists rely heavily upon conversation to develop a psychodynamic understanding of their patients. The younger the deaf individual is the less this form of communication or its alternate, writing, can be used. To substitute for limited interview data, it is necessary for the psychiatrist to have data from all people who are in close contact with the child. It is then the psychiatrist's job to decide among the following factors: (1) the altered behavior as a direct consequence of the deafness; (2) the behavior as a consequence of concurrent brain damage; (3) the behavior as a product of actual emotional disturbance; (4) the behavior as a product of disturbance in the family related to factor three; or (5) the behavior as a result of interaction between one or more of these conditions.

Occasional consultations with child psychiatrists do not provide what a competent group of professionals need for full psychiatric understanding of the deaf child. It is only after the child psychiatrist has worked with professional colleagues in the other disciplines for a period of time that the difficulties encountered in communicating between members of these various disciplines are solved. Understanding of the deaf child follows.

Finally, the direct effect of emotional disturbance in retarding language development has probably been exaggerated. We are in full agreement with Lenneberg's position on the influence of these factors.[33] Language competence unfolds transculturally on a biologically programmed schedule, which also crosses differences in personality. With the exceptions of the aphasic and the autistic child,* we feel the most reasonable position is to assume that if a child is not developing language as expected, one should not look to emotional disturbance in the child first. Poorly conceived communication models are more apt to account for improper language development than emotional disturbance.

---

*see chapter 4

Chapter 6

Oralism Only or Total Communication

Oralism is a restricted communication technique limited to speech, speechreading, writing, reading and amplification by hearing aids. Its one-hundred year history in America as the educational method for deaf children will not be discussed in this book. Relevant readings are listed in the bibliographic appendix. In this chapter, we will discuss the appropriateness of oralism to the task of teaching deaf children to communicate and compare it with the combined manual-oral system of total communication which includes the use of oralism as only one part of the total communication effort with the deaf child. In total communication, the language of signs and finger spelling are added. This gives the critical language information absent from the oral only method. It is a practical method for communication that can be initiated before the child is one year old. In one family, a deaf boy's younger hearing brother began using signs well before the age of one. The deaf mother of a deaf infant taught him the sign *eat* at five months of age. This method allows language to grow with the child—an absolute impossibility with oralism only.

Learning Patterns in the Young Child

Characteristically, young children have a limited capacity to become absorbed in learning tasks. One constraint on their learning is related to age. The younger the child, the less the cognitive capacity. Although to some this may seem self-evident, it is not uncommon to observe parents and teachers of young deaf children creating learning challenges well beyond the child's capacity. A second constraint is the ineffectiveness and lack of clarity with which learning challenges are communicated to the child. How careful is the parent or teacher to make clear what the child is expected to learn? Even many so-called educational toys have confusing arrays of challenges rapidly causing boredom or restlessness.

A two-year-old, for example, may touch on an area of interest for a few moments. After taking out and remembering what is meaningful, he will lose interest and want to move to another challenge. Of course, just moving rapidly from one place to another consumes much of the young child's time. They can become impatient or angry when such progress is impeded. Here there are also new skills in movement being practiced.

Oralism and Its Natural Constraints

In the typical oral instructional program, the parent is asked to become an active member of the teaching team, an idea more sound in principle than in practice. The parent must force the child to look at her face when he may not want to; it is hoped that he will "read" from the lips a configuration which is basically meaningless to him because the context is generally unclear. The parent is instructed to have the child look at his mother's face for the lip configurations a hearing child would hear and integrate as part of his language without even looking at the parent. It is interesting to note that the blind child develops language on the same time schedule as the normally hearing and seeing child. Observing lip movements is never a part of the blind child's language learning process. It never is for the normally hearing child either.

There are a collection of basic sounds deaf children are taught to repeat on cue, which they are capable of vocalizing naturally. Through associating these sounds with a seen lip configuration, and sometimes the corresponding objects or pictorial cues, the deaf child may learn that sounds he produces can have special meaning to hearing people.

A parent will be instructed to repeat a word referring to what appears to be the most obvious aspect of a situation in which the child is engaged. For example, the child chooses to pet a dog. "Puh" is a popularly taught phoneme. The mother may invite attention to her face and mouth "pet." What the child perceives on the lips is usually only a fragment of the entire word. Phonemically, it has three gross fragments: *Puh-eh-tuh.* The phoneme is the smallest unit of expressive language that conveys a difference in meaning. In this example, a change in any of the three component parts would create a different meaning: *bet, pat, pen.* Many such phonemic changes cannot be differentiated by the speech reader.

When teaching through oralism, one must always ask how the child will know the meaning of what the teacher or parent vocalizes. Often, the selection of words to be taught is random. Words have no natural meaning, and the child is not born with a vocabulary which he is able to articulate as his speaking organs mature. Sometimes, it seems as if the parent or teacher has a magical expectation that knowledge of the word already exists in the deaf child's mind, that he need only recognize it on another's lips to understand or articulate it. The meaning of words is determined only by recurrent usage within the environment and in relationship to the child.

The mother given the task of drawing the child's attention to her face to see a word on her lips that is related to his current activity must impose herself upon his natural play-learning patterns, often against his will. If she cannot impose quickly and with clarity, the communication will never achieve meaningfulness for him. The child's annoyance or anger resulting from interference with his play-learning patterns occurs frequently, but is often unheeded. The parent should interpret this to mean that she has failed to match the word chosen with the child's momentary interest or current capacity to understand. Some will regard it as "willfulness" on the child's part. Then, sounding clichés on how to deal with "willful" children such as: "The child must be made to learn" or "You must control the deaf child, not let the deaf child control you," some teachers and parents continue undaunted.

The basic process of teaching oralism is worth the effort, for it is one of many ways to communicate language information to the deaf child.

The trap lies in the failure of those who most avidly espouse this method to make known its realistic limits and use it as the only method. And, most distressing, is the naive assumption that the process duplicates or even approximates the language acquisition process in the normal child.

If oral instruction is done as part of the spontaneous transactions between mother and child, and careful control is exercised over the selection of words and situations, then a measure of learning can be achieved—an infinite distance, however, from full language capacity. If oralism forces the parent to divert the child from spontaneous learning and/or play, as it often does, then the converse will result. The child and parent will be so antagonized and frustrated by the intrusion that the whole process becomes painful and distasteful. It must be reemphasized that what seems to be random or play behavior in the child may, in fact, represent his pursuit or practice of a new cognitive or motor skill. Overzealousness for the oral method foreshortens the real gains by engendering the child's distaste. In addition, if it interferes with the unfolding of a gratifying, accepting, and loving relationship between mother and child, it creates a pathological situation. Some of the unspoken antagonism between older deaf children and their parents, no doubt, stems from these early difficulties. The parents experience far more pain later when the failures of the system are hard upon the parents' consciousness. Then it is difficult to examine objectively the years spent in oral training and admit that the initial commitment was a mistake.

In What Critical Ways Is the Combined System Different?

Sign language is a full language as it stands.[1] It does not have to be taught in parts like the phonemic learning of oralism. A sign is a complete meaningful clearly visible language symbol. Thus, it is easier to introduce into the parent-child or teacher-child system. It allows the richness of the parent-child relationship to develop unimpeded by a cumbersome communication technique. Signs are readily conveyed to the child, they have far less ambiguity. He can easily duplicate them. Sign language, finger spelling, and oral techniques complement each other. There are numerous parents who have used the combined method with their deaf children, found it effective, and have expanded its use in the family.[2] Siblings of deaf children, often still within their years of rapid language acquisition (ages two to thirteen), will learn sign language quickly and use it with their deaf brothers or sisters thus enriching and normalizing the child's interpersonal relationships. With sign language the deaf child is given access to peer learning, a necessary part of his development.

Average Language Attainment in the Young Deaf Child

By the age of five or six the average deaf child has little or no verbal capacity at his disposal, despite early oral training programs. For purposes of discussion, let us suppose that in a very successful oral program a deaf child five years old acquires a speaking vocabulary of two hundred words. However, he will have almost no knowledge of sentence structure. Many deaf children of five do not know the names of the foods they eat or the clothes they wear. Compare this with the hearing child who at the age of five is estimated to have a vocabulary from five-thousand to twenty-six thousand words[3] and the syntactical skills to combine them into meaningful sentences. It should be added that the vocabulary of the deaf child is often not understandable to people other than the parents or the teacher who has instructed him. Frequently, parents and teachers deceive themselves into believing that it is the words they speak that convey the meaning, ignoring the accompanying gesture which pantomimes the object or which indicates its location. For example, verbal phrases which are understood by deaf children like, "close the door," or "stand up," more often than not are used with the common natural gestures.

Demonstration Homes

Within the oralist movement, much attention recently has been focused on "model homes." In these homes, the young child is to be extensively exposed to language in a simulated home environment. In some centers, the method is utilized with children as young as one year. This experiment is publicized as an important development in the oral method. Superficially, the technique appears to have merit. Putting trained people into a simulated home environment should enhance the teaching of oralism. But, good window dressing lessens one's capacity to evaluate the real worth of the goods. When one considers the inefficiency of the basic method and the known language developmental sequences in children, much of the system's ostensible merit is lost. For the one-year old, it offers little for he is just moving out of the babbling phase and into a phase in which he is experimenting with more complex sound forms. These sound forms are the music of speech referred to in the previous chapter. For the older child, the model home environment serves to enhance oral accomplishments only by a small measure. If, however, a more efficient system such as the simultaneous method is used, these homes could provide an additional opportunity for learning language. One factor to consider carefully, however, is the cost: equipped with such things as major appliances, model homes can cost from twenty to forty thousand dollars. With shortages of public funds and the inaccessibility of many children to large urban centers, such demonstration homes show little promise.

The mother of a deaf boy made an interesting criticism of this concept. She contended that "a model home does not and cannot simulate real life." She saw the rationale for these homes opposed to the belief that "children make their greatest strides from the unexpected and unplanned." It was her impression that "children reared in contrived environments [i.e., the model home] become unnatural in their responses." To support her contention she offered the following vignette involving her five-year-old deaf son, Abraham.

One day the local high school nurse phoned to report that Frank, her older son, had been badly injured in a gymnastic accident. When she talked with the nurse, Abraham was nearby so she used manual signs and speech to help him become aware of the problem also. Then, taking him with her she continued to communicate about the crisis while they rode to the high school.

As Abraham observed his injured brother, and went along on the subsequent trip to the hospital, he had ample opportunity to compare the previously communicated information with developments he was soon to observe. He told his mother that Frank was "strong" and "brave" because, according to his logic, "Frank did not cry."

In the days following, Abraham apparently continued to reflect about the accident. (Children of Abraham's age are, of course, most concerned about harm to their body.) Not long after, Frank was able to leave for summer camp. He never wrote. An older sister who was spending the summer in France wrote frequently sending pictures and letters which were shown to Abraham regularly.

One afternoon Abraham, not feeling well, consented to nap and as a special treat was allowed to lie in Frank's bed. Abraham delayed going to sleep by a competent repertory of delaying tactics. His mother finally inquired why Abraham did not wish to sleep since he was obviously tired. Using his accustomed mode for communication, the combined system, Abraham replied: "Thinking of—dreaming of Frank; thinking of—dreaming that Frank is dead."

His mother communicated to him that this was not so, that Frank was at camp swimming, playing, and singing with friends. Abraham responded, "But Frank hurt—a deep cut over his eye—his elbow badly hurt—the doctor tried to fix Frank, Frank is dead." In spite of his mother's reassurances to the contrary, Abraham insisted that "Frank is dead."

His mother then recounted the events of that day to the child, but what happened after the doctor "fixed Frank" was not clear in the child's mind. Next, she helped him to recall how they took Frank to the train for departure and summer camp. Then she told him more of what Frank was doing at camp. Finally, and best of all, she ended with, "In four days we will see Frank at camp." With this clarification, he was finally able to sleep.

Thus through an unplanned, unexpected incident, Abraham was able to make real progress in a nonsterile situation.

Learning Through Other Modes of Communication

Difficulties inherent in teaching deaf children do not imply that the child is not absorbing and integrating various other important aspects of his environment. He observes activities inside and outside the home among parents, relatives, and family friends. He sees and uses some of the many things in his home. His developing intelligence allows him to interpret what he sees.

The child can perceive differences in role relationships—that "mothering" and "fathering" are qualitatively different. Observing and recording the routines of the home is an important aspect of his learning; his occasional violations of the order can lead to punishment, as can his curious and sometimes destructive explorations of some of the family's prized possessions. Although his mental functions are developing, his language is not.[4] The failure to develop the necessary accompanying and relevant language of his life patterns leads to progressive isolation from his family. The resulting frustration over this issue rises at times to intolerable heights, both for him and his family.[5]

Nonverbal Communication and Sign Language

In our discussion of the language of signs, we regarded its use as a natural aspect of man's capacity to communicate information about himself and his animate and inanimate environment using a variety of symbolic means. In our society, verbal speech is the most prevalent. Although efforts to develop a systematic understanding of nonverbal aspects of communication have been undertaken, present understanding is still in an early stage. Nonetheless, it has become increasingly evident that in nonverbal communication there is considerable information available.[6] A very simple example is a smile that accompanies "I like you." A frown or other angry expression accompanying those words would cause confusion over the actual intent of the communication, especially for the deaf child.

Very young children rely heavily on nonverbal communication. A parent can ask a twelve to fifteen month old toddler to bring her a familiar object. If at first the parent makes the request, taking care not to move her hands or gesture with her head, she will have less success than if she were to point to the child, to the object, and then to herself in one continuous gesture. This establishes the relationship of that object to her and the child. In this specifically nonverbal but important supplement to spoken language, the child learns what is demanded of him in the context of the accompanying language.

This is not to imply that without nonverbal communication speech will not develop. It is, rather, an attempt to emphasize the naturalness of gesture in the normal language learning process; it facilitates and enriches language learning for the child. As the child's language capacities mature, he will become rapidly less dependent on gestures. Later, the gestures will assume a different role in adult communication: they may convey emotion (banging with a fist upon a table); or, when words fail, gestures may help in pantomiming the object or action sequence; or they may illustrate quantity (the proverbial fish stories). In some cultures, gestures become a highly sophisticated and artistic form of communication. Native Hawaiian dances are an example; ballet is another.

Some parents actively discourage their hearing children from using their hands while talking. They teach that gesturing or even speaking with feeling is below the child's station in life. They feel that this form of communication is similar to talking with your hands, attributed to deprecated minority groups. However, when some of these hearing people are confronted with persons whose language they do not know, they either use their hands or sit like "stone snobs" who would prefer not to communicate at all than to use their hands and face.

The deaf child is more likely to attend to the nonverbal components of communication. Much nonverbal communication is heavily laden with emotional charge. Probably some of our capacity to assess positive and negative attitudes has an inherited biological basis, stemming from fundamental self-preservative and species-propagative behaviors. This capacity includes any one of a number of possible polarizations of attitudes: affectionate or antagonistic, friendly or unfriendly, warm or cold, receptive or hostile. For survival, man has developed methods to assess the intentions of his fellow-man. Adult deaf people (particularly the congenitally deaf with a profound hearing loss) probably attend more to these cues than the average normally hearing individual.

The deaf toddler soon becomes aware of gestures of displeasure which are often combined with some form of punishment such as deprivation of a desired object, the withholding of love, or physical pain. Gestures of displeasure clarify or emphasize the threat. The parent of the deaf child will early devise and use some basic gestural communication to guide the actions of the child, unless he is discouraged from doing so. Typically, the parent develops a few gestures which will come to have multiple meanings. One example is a gesture in which the parent holds both hands in front of himself with the palms up; he then moves his hands in a circular fashion. This multipurpose gesture generally means "where is it?" "what?" or "when?" It is universal to see teachers working in oral programs using a similar gesture to accomplish the desired communication. The overall meaning of this gesture to the child is that he perceives the parent is asking him to enter into a transaction in which the child will perform a desired act, such as getting an object, or saying a word associated with a particular act. Outside of a familiar situation, this gesture will have little meaning. A parent could not walk up to a deaf stranger, make this gesture, and expect anything but the deaf person's expression of bewilderment. Take, however, a situation in which the parent and the deaf person were walking side by side, and in full view of the deaf person the parent dropped his pencil. If then in such a circumstance the parent were to make this gesture, it could have the implication: "where is it?" and "would you be so kind as to help me find my pencil?" Context clearly defines this otherwise meaningless sign.

The young deaf child will ultimately come to understand that this sign has some value for him. While playing, the three-year-old child might remember that he wants his ball. He cannot find it and will come to the parent using this sign and conveying the concept of ball by pantomiming its use (bouncing or throwing), or perhaps say "buh" and link it with this multipurpose sign. If the parent knows where it is and she is so inclined, she may help the child find it. She cannot effectively communicate to the child the sentence, "I do not know where your ball is, but I will help you find it"; she can only start looking. That might suffice! But the parent may be busy with other children and not able to stop. She might answer the child with a shrug of the shoulders—probably the most common response to the original "where is it?" gesture, or just shake her head back and forth in a negative reply. She cannot communicate, "I'm busy with brother and sister and don't have time to stop now, but later when I finish feeding them, I'll be happy to look." The child understands that he is being refused when he perceives the mother's negative response, but he does not know why.

Even more trying for the parent and the child are the following situations. It is common for young children to become attached to a blanket, a pacifier, a bottle before bed, or a stuffed toy. These objects develop intensely personal meanings, especially cloth objects. They are called, *transitional objects* by child psychoanalysts because of their important role in the development of a child's relationships. For him, the blanket symbolizes the mother or maternal feeling. The child may cherish the blanket as much, or more, for its feel or smell, as for its appearance. The mother concerned over cleanliness may put this precious possession into the washer and then find her child standing by and fretting until the "purified" object is returned. How can the mother communicate to her deaf child that the blanket is not gone forever, but merely being cleaned?

If the family has a dog, he may be similarly attracted to the child's prized object. Dogs, during a family's absence on an outing of a few hours, may go to the various bedrooms and take objects which tend to absorb human smells: shoes, pillows, blankets, stuffed animals. A dog will use these objects more aggressively than a child, by chewing or tearing them. Let us assume a hypothetical situation. The family dog has taken the child's blanket and destroyed it. Although the child may see this, he will still demand the blanket when he is ready to go to sleep. The sensitive parent knows the symbolic value and the emotional need for the blanket and fully intends to replace it. But how then is this good intention to be communicated to the child?

Not being able to communicate good intent to a child can be one of a parent's most trying experiences. To accomplish it means that a parent must convey to the child the conviction "What I cannot do now I will do in the future." The parent of a hearing child might say, "Tonight you can sleep with this dolly instead; it's not as nice as your blanket to sleep with, but tomorrow—when you wake up in the morning—we will get in the car and drive to the store where we can buy you a new blanket." Ordinarily a hearing child will be only partially reassured by this promise, especially if he does not yet fully understand the concept of "tomorrowness." But the child will get the feeling that the parent is attuned to his special needs; and after some fretting or crying he will soon fall asleep. After arising the next day and having the previous evening's promise fulfilled, the child will incorporate an understanding of his parent's good intent.

A profoundly deaf child in a similar situation, without rudimentary language skills, will experience the loss of the blanket when he retires, but will only be able to communicate his wishes by crying. The sensitive parent may correctly guess that this is what the child is crying about. She may attempt to provide a substitute and may even plan to replace the object the next day, but she will be able to communicate only as much of this as demonstration will convey. The child will also see any anger on the parent's face, caused by frustration that may develop over this difficult situation. The angry expression will add to his grief the worry that he has offended his mother. Coupling this with the loss of the blanket, the representative of maternal warmth, the fear that he has offended his parent may make the situation even more overwhelming. Parents sensing realistically the precariousness of the situation may feel they are "walking on egg shells" when they simply attempt to satisfy some of their child's basic needs.

In some families, these sensitive situations result in extreme forms of behavior which leave the parent feeling overwhelmingly guilty. One parent of a deaf child described the "vicious circle that can result if the child cannot verbalize...a vicious circle of violence which I know is the common fate of the deaf child. He is violent—his parents are frustrated—they are violent. I've heard from parents and have seen it myself: terror builds upon terror—and the deaf child defies the parents to beat him, to beat him, and beat him—until the parent can take no more. This happens between four and five years of age."

To further demonstrate trying moments for a parent attempting to achieve understanding of her deaf child's plight, first consider how any young child communicates that he is in pain. Sometimes, the child will point to his abdomen to show that he has a pain there; or, he might pull at his ear and it means that he has a middle ear infection, although pulling at the ear is more often a habit, or a way of handling anxiety. As a hearing child grows older, he learns how to say "it hurts."

But what is the comparable situation for the deaf child? He may cry, point, or have temper tantrums. Articulating random phonemes such as "puh, puh" for "pain" serves poorly. Nothing so disturbs a mother as a pained child she cannot help. But there are simple remedies. When the child suffers pain from an obvious cause like a fall or a scratch, the parent can use the manual sign for pain: the index finger of one hand points to the index finger of the opposite hand. The fingers approach and are withdrawn from each other rapidly. This sign is performed over the injured area. Soon, the young deaf child will generalize this sign to any part of his body where he is experiencing pain.

Toilet training is an example of another situation that can create traumatic interactions between the parent and deaf child. Some parents have reported spanking the child for every accident and then placing him on the potty. Others have reported leaving the child on the potty for hours at a time. It is well-known that attempts to discipline through excessive violence often create oppositional behavior in the child. Toilet training will be delayed not accelerated.

The introduction of a nonambiguous sign for potty renders toilet training far more simple. The right hand is held in the finger spelled *T* position and moved from left to right. It is not at all uncommon to see the young deaf child having to communicate this need by holding himself or pointing to the genital area. Needless to say, a discreet sign is preferable. Thus, it can be seen that with the use of such uncomplicated signs, a parent will not have to resort to undesirable discipline or coercion which builds ill feeling and rigidity into the child's personality.

Determining the influence of limited linguistic achievement on the character development of deaf children has been a source of continuing inquiry. It has become increasingly evident that the introduction of useful and relevant signs with meanings reaching deeply into the basic structuring of language can profoundly influence the future personality development of the child. Words such as *how, what, why, when,* and *where* are not taught under the oral system until well past the optimal period of language learning. As a consequence, it is often very hard for deaf people to ask questions or for others to ask questions of them.

In the preceding few pages, we have attempted to relate our position on the need for a combined system of communication to a few situations that could occur in any home. Variations on the theme of a deaf child attempting to communicate feeling and desire and the parents' attempt at empathic reciprocal response are limitless. The variations derive from the particular nature of the home as structured by the parents and the kind of disability that the child has. The major goal with the deaf child is to sufficiently expand his capacity to communicate and be communicated with so that the home can be normalized as much as is possible.

There are over 2000 formal manual signs. There is not a one-to one correspondence between the number of situations that can be communicated about and the number of signs available. Meaning does not derive from the word itself but from the context in which the word, sign word, or sign phrase is used. Later, usage in context comes to be a permanent part of the linguistic structuring of the individual signer. One criticism of sign language has been its lack of correspondence with formal English structure and usage. This erroneous idea comes from the generally poor understanding of the formal properties of all nonverbal communication, including manual language. Combining formal signs with finger spelling does allow the use of nonverbal communication according to formal English syntax. Where signs are not known, words can be finger spelled. However, since the child's capacities to spell, finger spell, and read lag behind his ability to speak, signing and finger spelling do not always convey a complete communication sequence. Currently, there is much effort directed toward inflectional refinements of formal signs: tense endings, plurality, and irregular verbs. The irregular forms of the verb to be (were, are, is, was), and to have (had, has), can now be signed in a formal manner. It has been discovered that the young child—around four to five—already has the linguistic capacity to understand and transmit these irregular verb forms using formal signs.

In concluding this section, we would like to discuss some additional signs that we consider of great usefulness in establishing adequate communication with the young deaf child and which bear on his future adaptation and character development.* We will omit a written description of these signs, and refer the reader to standard works on sign language.

The first sign we wish to discuss is the sign for "help". This sign permits the child to indicate to the parent, or others, that he is in need of some assistance or that he is willing to offer it to others. The need for help can arise either from distressing internal states or from some external circumstance unnoticed by the parent, or which the parent has not perceived as troubling to the child.

Of particular importance is a way of indicating to the child that he must wait when he has requested that the parent do something for him, such as a request for food. The sign "after a while" permits the parent to indicate that she will honor his request as soon as she is able, but that time is "a little while" in the future. Thus, the child makes a request, the parent signs "in a little while"—implying "yes," but in a little while—and the child learns by experience that his request will be honored. Sometimes, a similar occasion will call for the sign "to wait." This strikes at the heart of a basic problem in the lives of deaf children and their parents. Deaf children are prone to have temper tantrums resulting from misunderstanding good intent in the parent. Most deaf people eventually learn to deal with the frustration of not knowing when and if a request will be granted by simply suppressing their anger. Unfortunately, such efforts bind energy that could be available for constructive pursuits.

Additional signs of considerable importance for the child's development are signs meaning "to share" and "to give." A mother conveying to the child that he must, or should, share with a brother, sister, or friend; or the mother's offer to share something with the child helps move the child away from an egocentric social position. Additional movement from an egocentric social position is achieved by providing signs for conveying emotional states such as happiness, sadness, or anger. Expansion of communication possibilities converts communication from demonstration only of feeling to a beginning incorporation of signs for concepts into the individual's linguistic system.

Signs that offer reward for the child are an excellent way of reinforcing desirable behavior. A parent can not offer the child a cookie or a hug on every occasion of a desired action. "Good boy (girl)," "right," and "yes," words that are used countless times each day in the life of the young child are of great help to the parent. Conversely, signs that convey displeasure or convey appropriate limits to the child, such as the signs for "no," "wrong," and "bad", are of great importance and help the child avoid punishment for every infraction of the house rules, major and minor. The usefulness of signs for "hurry" and "hot," "stop," and "more," are self-explanatory.

Fundamental in assisting the child in understanding the structure of

---

*The authors wish to express their gratitude to the following people for their suggestions on signs to include in this brief listing: Miss Marianne Collins, Miss Alice Moss, Mrs. Muriel Belson, Mr. Robert Van Dyke, and Mrs. Ethel Untermeyer.

his home are signs for "mother," "father," "siblings," and the sign for "home." As sibling names vary from home to home, these signs must be devised. Sometimes, they are created by finger spelling the first letter of the sibling's name near a part of the body that is in some way characteristic of that child — "H" near the head for Heidi with blond hair.

The following case history of a young deaf boy whose parents began early to use the combined method of communication further illustrates its efficacy.

At about two, Robert [a fictitious name] was found to have a severe to profound sensori-neural hearing loss. Like many rubella babies there were additional problems. One, a heart defect, was easily corrected by surgery. A second was a cataract, but the eye was too damaged to be rehabilitated.

When the child was brought to the Henner Hearing and Speech Center of Michael Reese Hospital, the mother gave the following written description of the child's personality: "Happy is what my baby always is. A very happy and smiling baby. At first, he was sick all the time, but after his heart surgery it was as if someone gave me a new child. He started gaining weight and doing all the things he was supposed to do earlier. He is very alert and picks up things quickly. At times, he gets frustrated and shows a little temper, but I believe this is because of his deafness."

Robert at three was described as being aware of sound; he could be conditioned to sound responses when wearing a hearing aid. However, he did not attend to conversational speech even with intense amplification. Progress in speech reading and speech was, for all intents and purposes, not identifiable.

Emotionally, it was not easy for him to become a member of the nursery school group. For the first four weeks he cried over separating from his mother. He could be encouraged to participate with the other children, however. He attempted to communicate through gestures. Initially, his attention span was limited. He could not remain at tasks for very long, but would get up and move about the room quickly until he seemed to exhaust a need to discharge his abundant energy. Then he would sit down and continue what he was doing.

Toilet training was late, and, therefore, he could not be accepted into a public school program for deaf children. In the meantime, his mother had started attending sign language classes and group therapy at Michael Reese Hospital. She became interested in the method, found it useful in establishing communication with the boy, and instituted its regular use at home.

Robert was an active participant in the nursery group. But, as time passed, he became more and more aggressive: when provoked by other children he would lash out. At times, it was not possible to identify the source of provocation and, therefore, it was necessary to "keep an eye" on him.

At the time of departure from preschool nursery after acceptance into a public school program, he was described as demonstrating good "fine and gross motor skills." In his intellectual development, he had responded well to reading-readiness work, and could write nine letters of the alphabet. Some very rudimentary mathematical skills were demonstrable and he was using sign language in the nursery to say such words as *cookie, juice, drink, time to eat, time to go home, come sit down, go,* and *good.* He was imitating finger spelling, but he had not yet demonstrated the capacity to use these letters spontaneously. Although he had gone through a period of very aggressive behavior, as he approached the end of his stay in the nursery he had learned how to get along better with other children. He was able to take turns rather than pushing, shoving, or demanding to be the leader. At times, when excessively stimulated or upset, he lost emotional control.

At the end of his first public school year, the teacher reported that Robert had demonstrated sudden progress in speech reading and was beginning to use his voice. He was observed to lipread such words as *hop, run, march.* He was one of two children who were reading.

Two months later, the child was visited in his home. A battery of tests was administered. Some were derived from standard intelligence tests under the supervision of the clinical psychologist. Some were based on materials used in the Michael Reese preschool project. The teachers described Robert as being very positive and enthusiastic in his approach to the formal testing situation. The visiting teachers were most impressed that he had started to speechread. Attention span throughout was excellent as opposed to earlier in the nursery school. When he completed a task, he was able to internally reward himself. [Looking to a teacher for affirmation of success is commonly seen in school children, not just in deaf children. It often indicates that the child has become more interested in the rewards than in the task at hand. The child's capacity to internally reward himself is a most critical aspect of the learning situation.]

Mother reported at the time of testing that not only had she been using a combined manual-oral system with the child, but the boy's father, brothers, and members of the extended family had also done so. He no longer demonstrated the outbursts of aggressive behavior which had earlier characterized his activities.

The mother at the time of this testing, raised a difficult question with the teachers. She observed that Robert is not always able to maintain the interest and attention of the boys in the neighborhood. She was able to see that this situation would get more difficult; he will experience greater isolation from them.

What stands out most strikingly in Robert's history is the mother's initial capacity to accept this child's most difficult handicap. This acceptance allowed the emergence of the boy's intellectual capacities. The mother's early insight that the cause of Robert's tantrums was his deafness enabled her to explain to herself much of the behavior-causing distress for parents of deaf children. The mother's acceptance of her son and the effective communication established with him went a long way toward relieving the temper outbursts. Although it is inevitable that this boy will experience some isolation from his hearing peers, as all deaf children do, he still has the safe harbor of a home in which he is able to communicate about his frustrations in relationship to other children in the neighborhood or school.

Examining the Deprecation of Sign Language

Why has sign language become a deprecated form of communication? Why is it that the gestural system of communication, beginning in infancy as a natural mode for communication, has fallen into disrepute among some parents and within much of the deaf education establishment? If the parents bring a very young child into an oral educational establishment, they are discouraged from using manual communication and encouraged to communicate orally with him even before a hearing child would employ verbal language. In some centers, oral instruction begins at one year of age.

We have no way of knowing what psychological motivations lie behind the original decision to derogate sign language. However, we can comment, on our observations of the use of the oral system in the classroom and on knowledge gained from conversations with current users and supporters of the system and from their publications.

The literature is of little help in understanding why oralism's adherents defend it so evangelically. It often reads more like propaganda and patent-medicine testimonials than scientific writing. There are testimonial reaffirmations of traditional stands using half-truths and deprecations of dissenters' views often with attempts to discredit their professional competence.[7] (For an additional discussion of the politics of oralism see "Dumb Children," The *New Republic,* August 2, 1969.) A letter to the *Volta Review* articulates well the criticism of the basic editorial policy of oralism's house organ.*

"Your recent editorial cautioning against overoptimistic or indiscriminate acceptance of new techniques and equipment for use with hearing-impaired children was timely and appropriate.
"We would, however, like to offer the following thoughts. As Daniel Fader of the Department of English of the University of

---

Volta Review, May, 1969, from Lazlo Stein, Ph.D., Director, Dr. Robert Henner Hearing & Speech Center, Michael Reese Hospital.

Michigan pointed out in a recent issue of the *Bulletin of the Council for Basic Education,* a field of study must meet two basic requirements to qualify as a profession. The first of these is a mastery of an intellectual discipline. Individuals engaged in the diagnosis, habilitation, or education of the hearing-impaired child should possess highly specialized and advanced skills. It is not our purpose here to enter the controversy of higher education as it is practiced today in certain fields, but rather to simply point out that the person whose training consists of survey, or how-to courses preparing him to be the equivalent of a general practitioner rather than a specialist, will in all probability not be the one who makes the major contributions we all desire. Furthermore, it is also very likely that this same individual will not be able to recognize such a contribution when it is offered.

"This brings up the second essential of a true profession—the critical voice which professionals raise in examining the work of their colleagues. As Dr. Fader points out, unlike the meetings or publications of other professions where the wolves eat the rabbits in one bite, the teaching profession (and I would include the fields engaged in work with the hearing impaired) encourages only rabbits and nobody eats anybody.

"A publication aimed at a professional group can adopt one of two editorial policies. One, it can have a strong editorial policy backed by a competent editorial review board and publish only those papers that meet the basic minimums of clarity of presentation and research design. The question of a controversial radical approach to a problem does not affect the decision to publish if basic scientific and professional standards are met. Such a position has the effect of reassuring the reader that an article meets an expected level of research competence although it in no way constitutes an endorsement or bestows a stamp of approval.

"The second editorial position is simply one that all papers relevant to an area of study will be published. In this instance, the author bears full responsibility for the scientific merit of his work and fully understands he is at the critical mercy of his colleagues. Several of the most prestigious journals in medicine, law and physics have such a policy. It is, of course, apparent that this type of editorial policy assumes readers are capable of making critical judgments and that only the ablest will survive in the profession.

"We are aware that *The Volta Review* has a diverse readership, many of whom rely almost exclusively on it for information and at least partial answers. While we agree with the statement that a claim to the total answer must be viewed with alarm and even suspicion, we hope the *Volta Review* will not adopt a categorical attitude, and thus deny its readers thought-provoking, or even controversial information. We urge the editors and readers of *The Volta Review* to be aware that insularity can be extremely destructive not only to a profession, but also to the individuals it attempts to serve."

Oralism's adherents will often intimidate or threaten parents to maintain their dominant position. The authors can document instances in which parents were told if they used sign language with their child, they could expect prejudicial treatment by school officials, to be kept on waiting lists excessively long, or to be excluded from the school system entirely. Threats are blunt only when the oralists are forced to explain or defend their position. This has been our experience as participants in a nursery program for young deaf children within a metropolitan area embracing a number of traditional programs. Few parents can stand these pressures and are eventually brought to their knees. Without sound and realistic information on the needs of deaf children, they never get up.

Consider the parents of a nearly five-year-old deaf girl with considerable language competence. She had been taught in the Michael Reese Program for over two years with a combined system. Her parents were informed by officials of a prestigious Eastern oral school that she had been "irrevocably damaged" and that "she may never learn to lipread" because they had not started oral training early enough. Such intimidating remarks are apparently "official policy." They are usually stated as follows: "The deaf child's future is limited unless he has learned to speak and lipread at an early age." Through statements such as these, the oralists pad their future against failure; they have already shifted the burden of guilt to the parents.

How the Myth of Oralism's Superiority Is Maintained

Several clichés are commonly employed to clinch and maintain a commitment to oralism. We must examine these for merit. Although we will examine them at the intellectual level using available research studies to objectify the evaluation, the implicit psychological messages must also be examined. The latter are the more influential in binding parents to the method.

"Every Child Deserves a Chance at Oralism"

This is perhaps the most common and destructive of these clichés. It implies, of course, that one form of communication is more important than another—as indeed it is—for the hearing child! The normal-hearing child does not elect nonverbal forms for communication. (Some autistic children ignore speech and are occasionally misdiagnosed as deaf.) This is supported by the fact that hearing children of deaf parents exposed to manual communication as the primary communication in their household become proficient speakers on schedule.

For the deaf child, speech does not have primacy. Speaking, for him, is a technique that must be learned and practiced, but is never mastered. The deaf child's natural communication—his natural language - is gesture.[8] Gesture is more reliable and infinitely more flexible. When his gestures are not molded into formal manual communication and finger spelling, they cannot serve as *flexible* language symbols. They are singular and unreliable, understood mostly by his parents whereas they could have been more reliably functional with intelligent channelling into formal manual communication and finger spelling.

Two sociologists at the University of California, Aaron V. Cicourel and Robert J. Boese, have developed a logical and convincing theoretical position regarding the importance of the deaf child's primary or native language system.[9] They state that because a deaf child cannot monitor the auditory feedback from his own vocalizations, he cannot make changes in that output in the course of a conversation. He cannot, therefore, "acquire oral language as a native." It is only in very exceptional instances that a deaf person can become a native speaker of an oral language. They point out that many oral teachers of the deaf are totally unaware of the importance of "native signs" in the child's perception and interpretation of his environment. These investigators assert that all deaf children convert whatever they are taught to their native language system.

Generally, the oral teacher assumes "that she is teaching this child his native language because he is learning to use his vocal chords, his oral cavity, his tongue, his lips, in order to communicate as 'normal' people do. But what the oral teacher of the deaf is doing is to teach this deaf child a second language." This second language will be added to the native language system but will not replace it.

The above is a very brief synopsis of a carefully outlined and elaborated theory. It has great importance to anyone interested in the language development of the deaf child.

During the many years that the deaf child is awarded his "chance" at oralism, the golden years for language acquisition are dissolving. As we demonstrated in the preceding chapter, language competence arises in an orderly manner. The right things must occur at the right time; they cannot be recovered later. Losses of learning opportunities in childhood are neither retrieved nor replaced; their absence at best may be understood.

There are a number of schools for the deaf with manual programs. Many deaf children must enter them with a sense of relief; they are freed to communicate in a manner comfortable to them. The children placed in these programs are regarded as dropouts from oralism. They are labelled with a variety of indecorous terms: "slow learners," "aphasics," "retarded," "oral failures," "willful," "emotionally disturbed," et cetera. Parents having been conditioned earlier to the "primacy" of oralism may regard placement of their child in a manual program as a signal of failure. "He has had his chance at the best; he has failed; he is not the best."

"If the Child is Taught Finger Spelling and Sign Language, He Will Never Learn to Talk"

This second cliché is as common as it is destructive. For over one-hundred years this misconception has paved the way for the deaf child's "chance" at oralism. Its corollary is, "Not only are manual communication and finger spelling second best, but they interfere with the development of first best."

There are now a number of research reports which conclusively disprove these traditional views. One is the now well-known study conducted at the University of Pittsburgh, sponsored by the United States Office of Education and published in 1964 (see table I). In it, deaf children of hearing parents were compared with deaf children of deaf parents. In the latter group, sign language was used with the children from an early age. Among the major conclusions of the study was the discovery that *early manual communication does not retard the development of deaf students' speech.* Thus, the shopworn and tired indictment that children who use manual communication will not learn to speak as well as those prevented from using it has been conclusively contradicted.

An especially interesting finding of the Birch and Stuckless study, in regard to the effect of sign language on speechreading ability, is that the deaf children of deaf parents scored slightly higher than the oral only group. Judgments made on the written communications by a panel of judges again showed the edge in the former group. On evaluations of social adjustment, there was little difference, only a slight tendency in the direction of the deaf children of deaf parents.

Deaf children of deaf parents have greater academic and social success than deaf children of hearing parents. The reasons are somewhat obvious. A home in which a deaf child has an acceptable way of communicating with his parents allows for necessary exchanges of information about feelings and the environment. Such information goes a long way in enhancing that child's chances of success in "the hearing world." The early use of manual communication facilitates the development of normal sentence structure which few deaf oral children have. This skill has long-range implications. There are many critical words that help frame thoughts and obtain information that are easily "signed" and are readily transferrable to the written or spoken word. For example, words such as *which, but, why, idea,* and *thing.* These are included much later in the oral deaf child's training.

The work with deaf children at Michael Reese Hospital demonstrated that when manual language is included as an integrated part of the communication with the child, the child can utilize all means for communication that are understandable to him.[11] The child responds to communications he understands and enjoys doing so. Children need no special rewards other than experiencing successful, gratifying communication.

The latter point cannot be sufficiently stressed. The assumption that the child must receive external rewards to motivate him in performing learning challenges is one of the influences on education attributable to the theorists of *operant* behavior. There is the further assumption that he will learn better when such a reward is provided. When these tasks are performed with children, a favorite reward is chocolate pellets—one at a time. In the average home, chocolate and every other confectionery creation is usually abundantly available. The candy offers little intrinsic reward and can be vigorously rejected by disturbed children. Beyond the mundane as-

Table 1

Results of Early Manual Communication

Investigator	Sample	Results
a) Meadow (1968) [*a]	56 deaf children of deaf parents (manual group) 56 matched deaf children of hearing parents (oral group)	1) Manual group better in reading (2.1 yrs.) 2) Manual group better in math (1.25 yrs.) 3) Manual group better in overall education achievement (1.28 yrs.) 4) Manual group better in social adjustment 5) No differences in speech and lipreading 6) Manual group better in written language
b) Vernon and Koh (in press)	32 pairs of genetically deaf children matched for age, sex, and I.Q. Manual group had deaf parents, oral group had hearing parents	1) Stanford Achievement Test Scores a) General average - Manual group better (1.44 yrs.) b) Reading average - Manual group better (1.39 yrs.) c) Para. mean. - Manual group better (1.57 yrs.) d) Vocabulary - Manual group better (1.19 yrs.) 2) Written language - Manual group superior at .002 level of significance 3) No differences in speech intelligibility, speech reading, or psycho-social adjustment
c) Stuckless and Birch (1966)	105 deaf children of deaf parents (manual group) 337 matched deaf children of hearing parents (oral group)	1) No difference in speech 2) Early manual group better in speechreading 3) Early manual group better in reading 4) Early manual group better in writing 5) Early manual group possibly better in psycho-social adjustment
d) Montgomery (1966) [*b]	59 Scottish children	1) Exposure to, use of, and preference for manual communication did not negatively affect speech or speech reading skills

Table 1 *(continued)*
Results of Early Manual Communication

Investigator	Sample	Results
e) Stevenson (1964)	134 deaf children of deaf parents (manual group) 134 deaf children of hearing parents (oral group)	1) 90 percent of manual group did better than matched oral students 2) 38 percent of manual group went to college versus nine percent of oral group
f) Quigley and Frisina (1961)	Sixteen non-residential deaf children of deaf parents (manual group) Sixteen non-residential deaf children of hearing parents (oral group)	1) Manual group better in vocabulary, in speechreading and better in educational achievement. Oral group better in speech.
g) Hester (1963)	Deaf children in New Mexico School for the Deaf. One group had fingerspelling beginning at school age, one group taught orally.	1) Fingerspelling group superior on standardized achievement tests.
h) Quigley (1969)	Sixteen orally educated deaf children matched with sixteen combined orally and manually educated deaf children.	1) Combined manual oral children did better in language, speechreading, and general academic achievement.
i) Denton (1965)	The academic top ten percent of deaf children ages twelve, fifteen, and eighteen from 26 schools for deaf. Manual group had deaf parents, oral group hearing parents.	1) Mean achievement test score of manual group 8.2, of oral group 7.7.

*Ⓐ The sample size varied some depending on variables measures.

*b This study did not specifically involve preschool manual communication.

pects of this approach, evolving from work originally done with rats, is the violation of more sensitive and sophisticated principles of human development. Had these external rewards been necessary at each point in the learning process of children, mankind might never have left the babbling stage. In essence, the child cares most that he learns how *to do* capably and that his curiosity is satisfied. How he learns is often of greater interest to the parent or teacher, than the child.

Another major study on the effects of early manual communication was conducted by Kaye Meadows.[12] She found, using matched groups, that the deaf children of deaf parents who were exposed early to manual communication were superior in reading, mathematics, written language, overall academic achievement, and social adjustment. There were no differences in speech and speechreading skills. (see table 1.)

In somewhat less comprehensive studies or those involving smaller groups,[13] it was found that thirty-eight percent of the deaf students exposed to early manual communication went to college compared to only nine percent of those who had strict oral early training. Two other studies,[14] again using matched groups of sixteen cases each, found the oral groups inferior in educational achievement. One of them reported that the speech reading of the manual group was superior.[15] The other investigation showed no differences in speech reading. One of these studies, however, gathered data on speech intelligibility indicating that the oral group did do better.[16] In yet a third related study, Montgomery in Scotland found that exposure to the use of and preference for manual communication did not negatively affect speech or speech reading skills.[17] In fact, there was a tendency for proficiency in speech to be correlated with manual communication.

The existing research unanimously reports superior linguistic and academic achievement for children exposed to manual communication or combined manual-oral communication in preschool years. The studies which obtained data on speech reading show the manual groups were equal to or better than matched oral samples. Except for one sample, both groups produced equivalent speech performance. Psychosocial adjustment test measures favored the manual group.

"The Deaf Must Choose Between the Hearing World and the Deaf World"

This cliché presents an artificial division which has been used to frighten parents into unrealistic programs and to justify outlandish educational endeavors.[18] Actually, it is not an either-or matter. Deaf adults generally work with hearing people. The selection of their work is task oriented, and deaf persons at work usually speak infrequently. Most deaf persons write to avoid confusion when crucial information must be exchanged. Socially, deaf adults prefer other deaf people; ninety-five percent marry among themselves.

The Oral Establishment — Who Belongs?

Some of the controversy over the oral and manual methods fits neatly into traditional dress: conformists equipped with a pat method to believe in and preach versus the nonconformists willing to give something novel a try. But the problem is deeper than this; it relates in part to why the individual chooses to work with deaf people. Many have had deaf relatives. Many teachers of deaf children have deaf children of their own. This is a particularly difficult situation. Many of these teachers have been confronted by the failures of the oral method in their own child and other children, but must continue to teach orally. They find themselves having to support an establishment view which they recognize has failed. Some learn sign language surreptitiously and use it with the child in the home. Others, thankfully, are more courageous and do not "go underground." It is hard to imagine a more painful and pitiful dilemma for a mother than being made to feel guilty over the wish to communicate with her child.

Among those working with the deaf who have deaf parents, there is more active support for sign language. They have grown up with it and are "bilingual." Even though spoken communication is not their "native tongue", their speech developed on schedule. They began using manual communication with their parents before they were one year old. It is common for such children to have recognizable finger spelling skills at the age of three or before.

Many avid supporters of oralism are well into middle-age and beyond. As is well-known, such times of life are typically associated with conservative conduct. These people enjoy an earned degree of respect and power in the field, and they tend to view a new method as threatening their position in some way. Those rigidly adhering to a system beginning to crumble do, indeed, have something to fear; they cling to a sinking ship. For those in the conservative years who recognize that changes are necessary, their position becomes more secure as they change gracefully with time and capitalize on the wisdom that age should bring.

There are even deeper roots to the rigid adherence to oralism. To spend so much time extracting a few recognizable words from a deaf child at the expense of more profitable, gratifying, and successful activities, a teacher or parent must have deep psychological commitments to the need for spoken language. That is, the significance of adequate speech has been *overdetermined;* i.e., it has assumed unrealistic importance for the teacher or parent. The reasons for such overdetermination are deeply buried in the individual's psychology.

There are other factors. The deaf child is completely, or almost completely, under the control of the educator; he is captive to the system and its proponents. The natural will of the child is subverted to the system. When a deaf child rebels and allows himself to express his impulses, he is regarded as an enemy; he may be expelled lest other children are lured into the natural expression of impulses. One cannot help but think that in many instances, those willing to carry on in such a system cannot love children very much, for such tactics subject the child to untold sufferings to support a system which is the creation of the hearing and not the deaf man.

All who operate within the oral establishment do not have the same background or beliefs. But, when all operate within one philosophical framework administratively implemented through an educational system, .

then the system itself possesses all of the traits. This collective identity is what the parent confronts as she matriculates her deaf child into academic and social groupings. Those who subscribe to the system as a whole assume responsibility both for the good and the bad.

Unheard voices of protest also are votes of confidence. To recognize what is bad in a system, and to continue to support it, has ill-effects familiar to all. For example, air pollution has plagued the residents of industrial urban centers for many years. Yet no pressure was brought to bear on the industries responsible. Their goods or services were widely purchased and they continued to prosper.

Though the world of deaf children is really a tiny speck in "the sea of humanity" most of the social, educational, political, and economic problems are no less typical for them than the problems of mankind at large.

The Call for Proof

The efficacy of the oral method has never really been documented, yet one of the most typical responses from the oral establishment to discussion about the value of sign language is that *its* efficacy has never been demonstrated. A well-known political tactic is to direct criticism based upon one's own weakness against the opposition.

The inefficacy of oralism, documented by the abysmal educational and vocational failures of this system, is discussed in the next chapter. That sign language becomes the chief mode for communication of the adult deaf and of deaf children in programs where they are not punished for its use makes a very powerful statement for its efficacy.

Direct punishment or punitive attitudes may be less common now than previously. It has been documented that one of the more well-known institutions for training deaf oral children placed bags over their heads for using their hands in communicating.

One parent observed her son's teacher digging her thumbs into his back because he did not sit down immediately when told. A college student working with an oral teacher during her community service work observed the teacher hitting the deaf children; yet, the woman is described as "a nice person." (She probably is under less frustrating circumstances.) The authors observed an experienced teacher strike a boy on the head with her knuckles when he gave a wrong answer. Although she was lavish in her praise when the boy succeeded, one wonders about the child's willingness to take chances when he knows that punishment is on the way for any mistakes. Another commonly observed maneuver is to forcibly jerk the child's chin toward the teacher's face to "see words" if he looks away.

One of the authors (E.D.M.) treated a seventeen-year-old boy who received his initial training at a deaf oral school. When he began to struggle over a word that could not be understood, he would grab his own chin. After much effort, he was able to accept the use of finger spelling. This opened up channels of communication through which poured torrents of ideas.

When this controversy occasionally reaches the public press, television, radio, or the theater, there are efforts made to suppress it. At the conclusion of its three year project with deaf people, the Michael Reese Hospital Research group under the leadership of Dr. Roy R. Grinker, Sr., held a press conference.[19] The national newspaper stories stated that the group advocated abandoning lip reading for deaf people. This was not the case. The group's recommendation was that lip reading and speech be deemphasized as the primary mode for communication and that a combined manual-oral approach be used. This unfortunate error did result, however, in many responses. One letter to the editor objecting to Dr. Grinker's misrepresented announcement in the newspaper story is quoted below.

> "I would like to express the shock of many parents and educators with Dr. Roy Grinker's advice to parents and teachers to no longer try to teach lip reading to deaf children.
> "He is apparently unaware of the many children and adults who have successfully learned lip reading to the extent that they can effectively communicate with normally hearing people without the use of signs.
> "His statement, 'They don't need to communicate with people who don't know sign language,' is gross defeatism.
> "If Dr. Grinker would speak with many deaf adults, he would find that they recommend early training in lip reading and the speech which can accompany lip reading.
> "Failures in our current educational systems cannot be overcome by substituting sign language for lip reading in the education of deaf children. If Dr. Grinker would visit the many schools where lip reading (speech reading) is taught, he would see that his advice could cut off many children from learning basic communication skills.
> "What is needed is the intelligent and organized efforts of skilled teachers and administrators working with modern facilities and equipment and assisted by interested and knowledgeable parents."

Replies to this letter were not printed by the newspaper. This demonstrates the difficulty of focusing proper newspaper attention on social issues. One reply, prepared by Robert Donoghue of the Educational Committee of the Illinois Association of the Deaf, is an excellent and moving statement by deaf adults on this controversy.

> "The criticisms voiced in reply to opinions regarding the failure of deaf educational methods currently being practiced in this country are, in the opinion of the Illinois Association of the Deaf, grossly unfair and misleading.
> "The author of the letter stated that it is bad advice to counsel parents and teachers not to rely exclusively on speech

reading (lip reading) in the academic setting. He also takes issue with the wisdom of teaching by the manual language method and suggests that Dr. Grinker hasn't done his homework properly in this field and is apparently ignorant of the signal success of the speech reading system practiced in the majority of the nation's school systems serving the deaf.

"Additionally, the author offers sage advice: to understand the deaf, the learned but uneducated Dr. Grinker would be wise to 'speak with many deaf adults' and learn that they recommend early training in speech and speechreading.

"He [the writer of the letter] would have us believe that the ghastly failures, the educationally atrophied children now being spawned by our school systems, cannot be prevented by switching from speech reading to manual signs. He does not believe that speech reading is the primary evil involved and suggests that the answer to the present state of affairs lies in securing 'intelligent and organized efforts of skilled teachers. . .working with modern facilities. . .'

"These arguments are patently absurd and unsupported by the facts. The acquisition of speech and speech reading consumes so much of the deaf child's time during his early formative years that he is almost in every case irrevocably retarded in his ability to read, write, and do mathematical problems by the time such activity is an accepted accomplishment among the hearing children.

"It has been shown that there is little physical dissimilarity between the hearing and the deaf child if the dysfunctioning auditory ability of the latter is ignored. The matter then boils down to the method employed to reach the deaf child during the educational process. Since the majority of the schools in this country rely on the speech reading method and the average language attained by the deaf is roughly the fourth grade level, it is rather well demonstrated to what source we can ascribe the current difficulties in teaching the deaf.

"The advice to Dr. Grinker to circulate among the deaf adult world is very timely in the opinion of this writer. In fact, it is advice that the author might well follow on his own. If he were to do so, he would discover something very interesting: even those of the deaf who are orally-oriented use the speech reading method when they must. . .they employ signs when they can. He would be surprised at the number of so-called oralists now working in organizations devoted to serving the deaf. . .and who insist on manual language in their councils on the grounds everyone present who is deaf can understand with clarity.

"The author of the letter cannot use the manual language. He cannot lip read. He has had absolutely no experience in the difficulties encountered among the auditorily handicapped. He has had very little contact with the adult deaf, has never offered to serve and study their needs, unlike many parents of deaf children who have given unstintingly of their time and money. He is a part of that vast majority of well-meaning but blindly led parents of deaf children who are determined that their offspring must resemble the hearing in every way possible in order that they may share in the same benefits later on.

"They might listen to the deaf themselves more closely. The deaf are pragmatists at heart. They are quite aware, thank you, that an excellent speech reader and linguist with a fourth-grade language level attainment is a drag on the technological market as it exists today. Those of them who have matriculated from a recognized college are largely self-educated individuals who had enough sense to avoid being entrapped in the artificial world created by proponents of the oral system, and who instead of concentrating on the development of speech, paid attention to the real reasons for attending school. . .to attain an education which would enable them to compete with their hearing peers at commensurate levels. *To these deaf, the penalty of living in a subculture is a small price to pay when measured against the innumerable benefits they have attained through the acquisition of a decent education.*

". . .parents of deaf children now in school systems might think this over carefully before they criticize. They might ask of themselves soberly, just what is it that they want and expect for their children? Do they want a caricature of a hearing child. . . one that walks, talks, and eats. . .and is several years behind educationally and often a butt to his hearing playmates? Or would they rather have their deaf children educated at the same rate as chronologically similar hearing children? It takes but fifteen minutes to teach finger spelling; two weeks will give a working mastery of the manual language, and by the use of the simultaneous method involving oral communication as well, speech reading need not be excluded. Speech reading by itself is so difficult to attain any degree of proficiency, and is so rarely profitable to the deaf unless they have some useful auditory ability remaining which can supplement visual intake that for all practical purposes, it is a shot in the dark. A parent who insists on the oral method exclusively is taking his child's future in hand and making a very poor gamble if past experience is any criterion.

"What will your child be. . .will he resemble you superficially, or will he be genuinely intellectually developed? You were too proud to come to us for the advice accumulated over the years; we are not too proud to go to you and to other parents as well. And remember, they're not our children!"

Unconscious Determinants

Finally in our search to explain the paradox of continued adherence to oralism, we look for clues to unconscious mental content. Oralism refers in this discussion to *a need to maintain the primacy of spoken language.* Paradoxes always suggest the existence of pertinent unconscious content, but such content is ordinarily inaccessible. A psychiatrist circumscribes conflict by examining the stream of conversation for paradox and contradiction. There is no greater paradox than the scene of children proven to be profoundly deaf, sitting with earphones in circles while "talked to" by a teacher.

The unconscious determinants establish the deep and adherent roots of commitment to ideas or methods. The greater the depth of the commitment, the more difficult is the task of altering commitment in the face of conflicting and compelling reality.

An inflexibility of character can prevent change in commitment. Inflexible individuals having once decided to pursue a given field have little capacity to make shifts. This difficulty may be predicated on limited intelligence; at times, it derives from a need to maintain order in the character structure to keep anxiety or inappropriate rage from becoming manifest. Control over rage must be very significant. An almost invariable consequence of many "discussions" with die-hard oralists about the combined manual-oral system is their unmanageable anger leading to a cessation of intellectual dialogue. Perhaps the rage derives from a feared threat to both social and professional position. But experience in examining irrational social and vocational positions leads one to look even further for symbolic meanings to these perplexing behaviors.

Now the unconscious mental causes of adherence to oralism, mentioned above, can be identified. There is apparently an implied threat to the control over one's infantile and primitive nature. Nonverbal communication is natural in the normal evolution of language competence. In hearing people, formalization of gestural language is very limited. There are said to be thirty formal gestures in our culture.

The infant's behavior is appropriately primitive. Initially, his behavioral responses are nondiscrete and he knows no shame for it. We know that many people feel uncomfortable in the company of infants and toddlers whose primitiveness can stimulate revulsion or total avoidance. *Some of the revulsion and avoidance is related to the individual's turning away from his own primitive past.* One major problem in recruiting more people to treat emotionally disturbed children results from a general turning away from one's primitive past. This operates in a subtle and difficult to demonstrate manner. It is demonstrable when one follows closely the course of their treatment of young children. Therapists can become anxious in close and extended contact with children and yet remain unaware of their own anxiety. They will, however, go through various maneuvers to avoid confrontation with primitive content.

Other sources of information about this phenomenon are primitive fantasies of mothers comfortable enough to relate private thoughts stimulated by their young children. For example, a mother unable to comfort the crying infant, may experience visual fantasies of injuring the child in retaliation. Some mothers are made so anxious by such thoughts that mothering responsibilities are seriously interfered with. Related to this are infant and child beatings resulting from the rage that the child's primitiveness can stimulate.

We are proposing that gestural communication is so intertwined with early infantile experience "left behind" in the unconscious that for some to consider its use threatens them with eruption of primitive thoughts and impulses they have long struggled to keep in check. The individual makes an unconscious association between primitive body language (gesture) and primitive behavior. Thus, the issue of how appropriate is the use of gesture for communication with the deaf child loses its direct relation to him. The intensity of one's commitment to oralism is rather a commentary on the individual's need to repress primitive aspects of his own personality.

When many teachers and parents undertake to orally educate the deaf child, the task is experienced internally as an effort in the service of overcoming one's primitive nature and the primitive nature of the deaf child. Any deviation of the deaf child from his intended mold threatens the individual with eruption of his own conflicts, often with associated rage.

Crude analogies are occasionally drawn between deaf children and animals. Our primitiveness is regarded as the animal part (therefore unacceptable) of our personality. It can be stated categorically that those not comfortable with the animal part of their own nature feel uncomfortable in free and unstructured relationships with children, especially deaf children.

Finger Spelling

Some who find sign language unacceptable support the use of finger spelling.[20] The Rochester Method combines oralism and finger spelling. Some have suggested initiating its use with the deaf infant. When employed too early, difficulties similar to the "pure oral" approach are encountered. It must be remembered that the child ignores language symbols which he cannot understand and work with. It does not further language development to finger spell to the child as he lies in the crib.

Some find finger spelling more acceptable than sign language, apparently because it is more directly related to written language. Conventional syntactical forms can be preserved with its use. Finger spelling can be used reliably with children from between the age of three to six and beyond with deaf children of average or better intelligence.

Writing

The use of the printed symbol as an alternate form of communication has merit for the child old enough to learn it. However a child does not begin learning to read and print until at least age three. Then he begins to match letters with letters, words with words, words with pictures, and so on. The paradox in the suggestion that writing be used as an alternative to oralism is that by the time a child begins to use it productively, the optimal period for learning vocabulary and syntax has passed.

It is most regrettable that deaf children generally are such poor readers, for in addition to being shut off from their sound environment, they cannot replace it in what would seem to be an obvious way—affording themselves the pleasures of literature. In some schools, reading is actively discouraged because of its alleged interference with the development of speech.

It is our firm conviction based on research evidence and clinical experience that there is not now a better method for the development of language in the deaf child than the combined manual-oral system. It is the only system that can be introduced at a very early age that is effective, because it conveys critical nonambiguous language information as it is needed. Oralism, no matter how intensively or effectively it is taught, cannot match the efficacy of the combined system.

The goals to achieve through a realistic language program are a flexible parent-child relationship and a rich education made possible only by adequate communication. The parent can then more effectively cope with the very special kinds of problems the deaf child has and can provide an effective link to the world beyond the home. His social and educational adaptation can become more flexible and rewarding.

The major effect of the inability to verbalize with the child early leads to isolation of that child from the parent. Other than communication around basic needs, there is little effective communication with these children. Parents, however, develop numerous and varied fantasies about these children and their understanding. The more subtle aspects of one's culture and feelings that are communicated by language are lost to the deaf child. This isolation often does not stop when the child develops some verbal vocabulary. There is a rapidly widening gap between the developing child and the psychosocial and psychosexual demands that are placed upon him.

To help parents employ sufficiently a combined manual-oral system is a major problem. Most parents have suspicions that their child is deaf by his sixth month. Parents do not act appropriately on this knowledge because of resistance to accepting the implications of the deafness and the general failure of society to provide adequate social work, psychiatric, and psychologic services. Rehabilitation cannot be started if they do not acknowledge their child's disability.

Parents initially do not see in their child's future the isolation from his hearing parents and siblings, neighborhood friends, and even deaf peers with whom he communicates in only the most rudimentary manner. In most programs for deaf children they are encouraged to communicate by a means which, because they cannot hear, is unnatural for them. There is a danger of generalizing this difficulty to their own self-concept. Their natural language is unacceptable, therefore, they are unacceptable. The early years when gesture is being discouraged are when the child's thinking is more literal. If parts of his behavior are rejected, he can feel rejected as a total person.

One of the authors (E. D. M.) once asked a profoundly deaf ten-year-old boy if he knew sign language, whereupon the boy answered "No, that's for deaf mutes." It is as if he regarded himself as a hearing person "temporarily out of order," who with the proper concentration on speech and speechreading would become like everyone else, like his parents' and teachers' fantasies would have him become. Thus, the children and the parents share a delusional system with eventual "recovery" from deafness at its core. Deaf children, their parents, relatives and friends, and the child's teachers all participate in the perpetuation of this tragic delusion.

Chapter 7

Outcomes

In this final chapter, we will examine the results of traditional educational and habilitative programs. The successes or failures of deaf adults are the ultimate measures of the effectiveness of present practices with deaf children. Unfortunately, the process, rather than the end product, has too often been the primary concern of professionals in the field of deaf education. As stated previously, most of those who structure and provide education for deaf children have little or no knowledge of or contact with deaf adults. Thus, they have conveniently isolated themselves from the results of their programs.

Intelligence and Cognitive Capacities

In the past, deaf people were called "dumb" and thought to be undeserving of ordinary rights. This view was supported by some ancient scholars including Aristotle. Systems of justice such as Roman Law incorporated this erroneous concept. In more modern times, initial efforts at testing intelligence seemed to confirm those beliefs since appropriate modification of the tests to account for the effect of deafness on language development, necessary to achieve valid testing, had not yet been done. Now with proper intelligence tests, it has been conclusively demonstrated by over fifty independent studies that deaf and hard of hearing people have essentially the same distribution of intelligence as the general population (see table 1). All the available evidence demonstrates that there is no direct relationship between hearing loss and intelligence.

Deafness does not necessarily imply impaired intellectual development. The occasional association of hearing loss with "dumbness," by the lay public and some professionals, is without basis in fact. This fallacy rests either upon the misconception that lack of speech means immature cognitive abilities or upon the equally invalid assumption that errors in the writing of deaf and hard of hearing people reflect negatively on their intelligence. Such errors simply reflect the lack of adequate opportunity to learn language through hearing it.

Another and perhaps more sophisticated fallacy is that deaf and hard of hearing people are less capable of abstract thought.[1] Research on the relationship of language to thought processes shows clearly that capacity for abstract thought is no different among deaf people than among the normally hearing.[2] This point is best illustrated by the large number of deaf mathematicians.

Educational Achievement

Educational achievement stands in sharp contrast with the facts on equal intellectual ability. Although a few deaf people are elected to Phi Beta Kappa or earn doctorate degrees for example, the average deaf adult

TABLE I

INVESTIGATIONS OF THE INTELLIGENCE OF THE DEAF AND HARD OF HEARING: 1930 TO 1967*

Reference	Sample and Age (Yr.)	Measuring Device or Test	Results
Peterson, E. G., and Williams, J. M. (1930)	466 deaf, 4-9	Goodenough	Average retardation: 1 10/12 yrs.
MacPherson, June, and Lane, Helen S. (1932)	61 deaf children	Hiskey, Randall's Island Series	Mean IQs: 116.62 and 113.87, respectively
Meyer, M. F. (1932)	132 deaf, 5-20	Lectometer	Deaf scored slightly lower
Shirley, Mary, and Goodenough, Florence (1932)	406 deaf, 6-14	Goodenough, Pintner Nonlanguage	Medians 87.7 and 98.4, respectively
Lane, Helen S. (1933)	43 deaf preschoolers	Randall's Performance	Medians: 96 (in 1931); 97 in (1932)
MacKane, K. (1933)	Deaf children	Grace Arthur, Pintner-Patterson, Drever-Collins, Pintner Nonlanguage	Retardation: 1 yr. or less; Pintner: less than 2 yrs.
Lyon, V. W. (1934)	Deaf children	Grace Arthur, Pintner Nonlanguage	Medians 92 and 84, respectively
Bishop, Helen M. (1936)	90 deaf and hard of hearing	Grace Arthur	Normal distribution
Peterson, E. G. (1936)	100 deaf, 5 7/12-17	Kohs Block Design Minnesota Preschool,	Mean IQ: 92.5; range: 54-156; scores clustered around 80 and 100 with 17% at each
Scyster, Margaret (1936)	50 preschoolers	Merrill-Palmer, Pintner-Patterson	Deaf showed no retardation

Study	Sample	Test	Results
Lane, Helen S. (1937 and 1938)[4]	250 deaf, 5-19	Lectometer, Randall's Performance	Equal ability; median: 97.6 Deaf mean: 105-122; depending on scoring method
Lane, Helen S. (1938)	50 deaf preschoolers	Drever-Collins	Deaf scored appreciably lower, with congenitally below adventitiously deaf
Springer, N. N. (1938)	330 deaf, 6-12	Goodenough	Same results as normals; age at onset not a factor
Streng, Alice, and Kirk, S. A. (1938)	97 deaf children (4th and 5th graders) 1,404 hard of hearing 1,556 normal	Grace Arthur, Chicago Non-Verbal Pintner IQ Test Pintner IQ Test	Mean: 94.7 Mean: 101.6
Pintner, R., and Lev, J. (1939)	315 hard of hearing	Pintner Nonlanguage	No significant difference compared to normals
Zeckel, A., and Kalb, J. J. (1939)	100 deaf children	Porteous Maze	"Backward" IQ
Burchard, E. M., and Myklebust, H. R. (1942)	189 deaf children	Grace Arthur	Deaf IQ is average; no significant difference between congenitally and adventitiously deaf
Johnson, Elizabeth H. (1947)	57 deaf children	Chicago Non-Verbal	Six groups with mean IQs of 73, 69, 69, 78, 85 and 99, respectively, from pregrade 2 to grade 3
Kirk, S. A., and Perry, June (1948)	49 deaf and hard of hearing children	Ontario, Nebraska	No conclusion re relative intelligence
Myklebust, H. R. (1948)	Deaf children	WISC Performance	Mean IQ:101.8
Glowatsky, E. (1953)	24 deaf and hard of hearing, 7.5-15.7	Goodenough	Mean IQ:98.46
Graham, E. E., and Shapiro, Esther (1953)	20 deaf children	WISC Performance	Mean IQ:96.1
Ross, Grace (1953)	61 deaf, 3-10	Ontario, Hiskey, Vineland	Mean IQs: 104.6, 104.8, and 94.7, respectively

Investigator	Subjects	Test	Results
DuToit, J. M. (1954)	289 deaf children from different schools and 180 from same school	DuToit's Nonlanguage Group Test	Mean IQ of 'different school' group: 98.53; mean IQ of 'same school' group: 99.96
Lavos, G. (1954)	90 deaf and hard of hearing children	Pintner General Tests, Chicago Non-Verbal, Revised Beta Examination	Correlation coefficients between tests ranged from 0.58-0.69; statistically significant
Frisina, D. R. (1955)	3 midwestern schools for the deaf 380 normal children	Grace Arthur	9.2-12% below 79 in IQ
Hiskey, M. S. (1956)	466 deaf, 4-10	Hiskey	Mean IQs: normal hearers, 101; deaf, in mid-90's
Goetzinger, C. P., and Rousey, C. L. (1957)	101 deaf, 14-21	WISC Performance	Mean IQ: 101.9
Vernon, M. (1957)	97 deaf children	Goodenough	Mean IQ:90
Larr, A. L., and Cain, E. R. (1959)	248 deaf children 63 deaf children 77 deaf children	WISC Ontario Grace Arthur	Mean IQ: 97.8; range: 61-138 Mean IQ: 98.1; range: 52-129 Mean IQ:101.1; range: 61-147
Brill, R. G. (1962)	312 deaf, 5-16	WISC Performance	Mean IQ: 104.9
Mira, Mary P. (1962)	60 deaf preschoolers, mean age 4.77	Leiter, Hiskey	Mean IQs: 96.32 and 108.86, respectively
Anderson, R. M., Stevens, G. D., and Stuckless, E. R. (1966)	1,600 deaf children from six residential schools	Performance Scales	19% below 83 IQ
Vernon, M. (1966) Vernon, M. (1966) Vernon, M. (1967)	66 deaf children 39 deaf children 92 deaf children	Performance Scales Performance Scales Performance Scales	Genetic deaf mean IQ: 114 Rh deaf mean IQ:94 Postmeningitic deaf mean IQ:96
Vernon, M. (1967)	115 deaf children	Performance Scales	Premature deaf mean IQ:89
Vernon, M. (1967)	98 deaf children	Performance Scales	Postmaternal rubella mean IQ:95

Investigator experienced in the area of deafness at the time of research cited.

*This table reprinted from the *Journal of Rehabilitation of the Deaf,* 1968, Vol. 1, No. 4, pp 4-7.

Table 2

Studies of the Educational Achievement of Deaf Children*

Investigator	Sample	
Boatner (1965) and McClure (1966)	93 percent of deaf students in U. S., age sixteen years or older	1) 30 percent functionally illiterate 2) 60 percent grade level 5.3 or below 3) Only five percent achieve at tenth grade or better and most of these are adventitiously deaf or hard of hearing.
Wrightstone, Aranow, and Moskowitz (1962)	73 school programs for deaf representing 54 percent of deaf school children, ages ten to sixteen	1) Average gain in reading from age ten to age sixteen less than one year (0.8 months) 2) Average reading achievement of sixteen year olds was grade level 3.4 3) 80 percent of sixteen year olds were below grade level 4.9 in reading
Schein and Bushnaq (1962)	Gallaudet College population and estimates of other deaf college students	1) 1.7 percent of deaf school age population attend compared to 9.7 percent of hearing school age population
Babbage Report (1965, p. 23)	269 schools and classes, 23,330 deaf children, 76 percent of deaf school age children (90 percent of residential school pupils and 57 percent of private residential pupils. Day classes and school not represented)	1) Median average on Stanford of school leavers is 5.9 2) 13 percent of students "left" at age sixteen or before 3) About three percent were denied admission 4) Waiting list for residential schools was 3.6 percent of enrollment, for private school 48.5 percent

*This table reprinted from the *Journal of Speech and Hearing Research*, 1969, Vol. 12, No. 3, p. 548.

Table 3

Results of Oral Preschool Education

Investigator	Sample	Results
Craig (1964)	101 deaf children in control group, 151 deaf children in experimental group. (Western Pennsylvania School and American School.)	No significant differences in speech reading and reading after a few years in school.
Phillips (1963)	Preschool deaf children and controls from Eastern U. S. schools including Lexington School, American School, and others.	No significant difference between preschool and non-preschool groups in academic achievement by age 9 years.
Vernon & Koh (1970)	All graduates of the three year Tracy Clinic program matched with children who had no preschool at all.	Deaf children with early manual communication and no preschool were far ahead of matched children who had three years of oral preschool at the Tracy Clinic and whose families had counseling. Deaf children with no early manual communication and no preschool were far below the early manual group, and not significantly below the Tracy sample.

Table 4

COMPARISON OF EARLY MANUAL AND EARLY ORAL
PRESCHOOL AND EARLY ORAL DEAF CHILDREN
WITHOUT PRESCHOOL EDUCATION [1,3]

Variables	Children with Early Manual Communication and no preschool[2]	Children with three years of Tracy Clinic oral preschool education	Children with no preschool, but an early oral environment	Tests for significance of difference
Matching Variables				
Age	18.2 years	18.5 years	18.7 years	$F\,(2,66) = .29\ p{>}.05$
IQ	116	114	114	$F\,(2,66) = .29\ p{>}.05$
Stanford Achievement				
Test Scores				
Paragraph meaning	7.6	6.1	6.2	$F\,(2,66) = 3.60\ p{<}.05$
Word meaning	7.0	5.9	5.8	$F\,(2,66) = 2.50\ p{>}.05$
Reading Average	7.3	6.0	6.0	$F\,(2,66) = 3.51\ p{<}.05$
Total Stanford Average	8.9	7.9	7.8	$F\,(2,66) = 1.39\ p{>}.05$

Footnotes: 1. Table based on original research by Vernon, M. and Koh, S., Michael Reese Hospital, 1969.
2. Had deaf parents.
3. Based on twenty-three matched pairs.

is undereducated. This is a clear indictment of educational systems which have failed to develop the intellectual potential of the average deaf person. This lack of academic advancement also acknowledges the impediment to normal learning caused by severe or profound hearing loss.

There are a number of studies which document the educational failures of deaf youth (table 2). In the most extensive current survey of educational achievement (study a, table 2) which included ninety-three percent of the deaf students sixteen years or older in the United States, *only five percent of the students achieved at a tenth grade level or better. Most of this five percent were hard of hearing or adventitiously deafened. Sixty percent were at grade level 5.3 or below, and thirty percent were functionally illiterate.*

In an earlier survey (study b, table 2) on reading achievement covering seventy-three school programs and fifty-four percent of all school-age deaf children between ten and sixteen, eighty percent of the sixteen year olds were below grade 4.9 on the Metropolitan Achievement Test. Furthermore, the average gain in reading from ages ten to sixteen was only eight months as contrasted to the gain of six years for the average hearing child.

For additional reports document the educational failures.[3] Schein and Bushnaq's 1962 study (study c, table 2) shows the small percentage of deaf youth who are able to enter college. The percentage of the deaf population entering college has been declining, whereas the reverse has occurred in the general population. The other reports were the 1965 Babbage Report of the Secretary of the Department of Health, Education, and Welfare's advisory committee (study d, table 2): Herbert Kohl's 1967 monograph for the Center of Urban Studies; and Donald Moores' report. It is of special interest to note that Moore's report shows most of these other studies yielded spuriously favorable results because standardized educational achievement tests give credit for guessing and matching and thus "fail" to depict accurately the language retardation of deaf students.[4] Many of the students who were dropped from surveyed schools as academic failures were not even included in the sample, nor were many of the small isolated day classes around the country. Had the samples been more comprehensive, the results would have been even lower.

Parents are traditionally led to believe that preschool oral education may correct these distressing educational deficiencies. Research on the effects of oral preschool programs fail to support such claims. Two independently conducted investigations which included a large percentage of Eastern oral preschool programs (table 3) showed that when the children with oral preschool training had been in elementary school a few years, the effects of their training on their educational achievement had "washed out."[5] Their educational level was no higher than the matched group with no preschool oral experience.

The most striking of preschool studies is one on the educational achievement of deaf children who attended the three-year John Tracy Clinic program, tables 1, 3, and 4. The Tracy Clinic preschool not only includes intensive oral education for the children, but also extensive instruction and group and individual psychotherapy for parents. The Tracy Clinic is generally regarded as the finest and most comprehensive oral preschool program in the world. Graduates of this three-year preschool who later attended the California School for the Deaf at Riverside were matched on the basis of I.Q., chronological age, and sex with deaf children who had early manual communication because their parents were deaf. The latter group had no preschool training but did better on tests of educational achievement and language skills and were equal in oral skills. Deaf children with no early manual communication and no oral preschool scored as high on educational achievement tests as the children trained in the Tracy Clinic preschool program. Both groups were far behind those with early manual communication. Thus, manual communication used in the home proved far more valuable educationally than the best of preschool programs.

Interestingly, despite claims that Tracy children matriculate into public schools, an examination of the population of the California School for the Deaf, which serves Southern California, showed that half to three-fourths of Tracy graduates eventually attend this school rather than hearing schools. The Riverside school is exclusively for deaf children. Considering the mobility of the Southern California population, it is probable that many are in other residential schools. Describing the study of the "Tracy Children" is in no way intended to demean their program. The school is well-equipped and well-staffed with intelligent people. It is hoped that citing such studies will help them to shift their emphasis away from a preoccupation with speech and speech reading skills. Although their more recent emphasis appears to be on language development, the vehicle for communicating language information is still speech.

The gross discrepancy between what is effective for deaf children educationally, i.e., total communication, and what is actually provided them — a restriction to just oralism — grows from a strange paradox. The professionals in education, audiology, psychology, speech pathology, medicine and related disciplines are the ones who exercise primary control over the institutions and programs that control the educational and psychosocial opportunities for deaf children. But, few members of these professions have had more than superficial contact with adult deaf people. In fact, many college programs preparing professionals to work the area of deafness refuse to accept deaf applicants, and many schools will not hire deaf teachers to work with deaf children. Students are usually not provided an opportunity to learn finger-spelling and the language of signs. Thus, those professionals who determine in large part the educational, vocational, and psychosocial opportunities for deaf children have little or no notion of results.

While many educators of deaf children and some speech pathologists and audiologists are emotionally unable to accept and apply methods other than oralism, there seems to be, overall, an increasing willingness to consider the facts. In view of the proven inadequacy of existing systems, the need for constructive change is most evident. Education is crucial in determining all other psychological and sociological aspects of the lives of deaf people. Changes must be made in education first and foremost.

Communication

As a result of the difficulties in learning to speak when deaf, there are few prelingually deafened persons who develop speech that can be understood in most social situations. In the past, before the use of antibiotics, thirty to forty percent of deaf children lost their hearing after having developed speech and language. Today ninety-five percent are deafened prelingually![6] Many, if not most, professionals in deaf education and rehabilitation tend to ignore this fact and its implications. Their "business as usual" attitude continues unencumbered by reality.

Edgar Lowell's 1957, 1958, and 1959 studies conducted by the Tracy Clinic illustrated the problems inherent in speechreading.[7] Nondeaf college sophomores who had never studied speech reading were more successful at it than deaf persons to whom it had been taught throughout most of their school careers. The better performance by the nondeaf sophomores derived from their normal language base (phonetic, semantic, and syntactic), enabling them to determine by guessing the words they could not speech read. It is helpful to remember that forty to sixty percent of English sounds are homophonous: their formulation on the lips is identical to that of other sounds (see page 58). A person without an adequate language base to fill in the gaps understands very little. In fact, even the best speechreaders in a one-to-one situation were found to understand only twenty-six percent of what was said.[8] Many bright deaf individuals grasp less than five percent.[9]

Thirty percent of deaf children are functionally illiterate. Their average gain in reading from age ten to age sixteen is less than one year, and their command of expressive and receptive language is even less. Thus, communication by reading and writing is also severely limited for the majority of deaf persons. With more realistically designed programs, this need not be the case.

In summary, it can be unequivocally stated on the basis of the material presented above that most parents cannot communicate with their deaf children except at a superficial level unless they themselves learn manual communication. Very few parents do this and very few will if efforts to suppress such communication are successfully implemented by certain segments of the professional community. Thus, deaf children do not obtain knowledge of ethics, morals, and social codes, the importance of education, intelligent career planning, and so much else that parents ordinarily provide for their children.

School programs all over the United States are turning out a high percentage of deaf students who have no means of adequate communication. They have been, and are being denied peer, parent, and teacher relationships. The resultant knowledge which they have been denied will be available now and in the future for deaf children if they are provided a combined manual-oral education.

Due to the ineffectiveness of the current educational approach, vocational rehabilitation centers must first teach manual language skills to the deaf persons referred to them. Then educational efforts are made to fill in all that has been lost over the crucial early years. As adults, these deaf cannot be given all they were denied as children. Thus, many of them function in our society as isolates unaware of much of the world in which they live. This does not have to be and should not be the case; but until realistic adjustments are made to accommodate the communication problems of deaf people, the situation will remain.

Marriage Patterns

Ninety-five percent of deaf people marry among themselves.[10] The remaining five percent is composed generally of hard-of-hearing people, or people who lose their hearing later in life. In most cases marrying another deaf person is a healthy adaptation to deafness, and the marriages are usually stable.[11] There is a higher percentage of deaf unmarried persons as compared with the hearing population due, in part, to the higher number of deaf men.

That the majority of deaf people marry other deaf persons (including those who graduate from exclusive, expensive, private oral schools) and the marriages are successful further indicates that the deaf people are socially gratified in the company of those with similar communication modes and social problems. It is the egocentricty of professionals and parents which causes them to view this natural phenomenon as a failure. The cliche "they have not learned to live in a hearing world," heard again and again results in an unremitting emphasis on integration. This emphasis has not resulted from a realistic appraisal of the needs of deaf children and adults. It is an effort to superimpose inappropriate majority group values on a minority.[12]

Social Organizations

For obvious reasons, deaf adults have made conscientious efforts not to leave responsibility for their welfare in the hands of the hearing. They have founded effective organizations to meet social, psychological, and political needs. These groups are an integral part of their lives. The most prominent is the National Association of the Deaf (N.A.D.) with over 10,000 members. There are N.A.D. branches in every state and a permanent office in Washington.* National meetings are held regularly. The organization is a constructive force in the lives of deaf people, actively protecting and representing their interests. It serves, in addition, to organize cultural, athletic, and social events. In recent years, the N.A.D. has conducted research in deafness and contributed to parent education. The association's excellent publication, *The Deaf American*, is widely circulated and of interest to deaf persons, parents, and professionals.

The American Athletic Association of the Deaf conducts regional and national sports tournaments. Teams travel all over the United States to compete; national championship awards are made. Every four years an

---

*The central office address of the National Association of the Deaf is 814 Thayer Avenue, Silver Spring, Maryland 20910.

international deaf olympics is held. All of this is organized and financed by deaf persons.

The National Fraternal Society* ("the Frat"), with a membership exceeding 10,000, is both a fraternal organization and an insurance company. It was originally established because of discriminatory practices toward deaf persons trying to obtain life insurance. Run by the deaf, it has become very successful. It continues to provide life insurance at reasonable rates for its membership. In addition, the society conducts social functions throughout the United States.

A unique new organization in the deaf community is the National Theatre of the Deaf. It was initiated through the efforts of the well-known psychologist in deafness, Dr. Edna Levine, and by Dr. Boyce Williams, a deaf man and a ranking administrator in the Rehabilitation Services Administration of the Department of Health, Education, and Welfare. The National Theatre repertory group has performed on Broadway, the Lincoln Theatre in New York City, on nationwide television, in legitimate theatres throughout the country, and before college audiences. The actors are deaf and perform using sign language with nondeaf actors reading aloud simultaneously. This new acting form has received outstanding reviews and has attracted wide interest from both deaf and hearing theatre goers. It has greatly enhanced the general public's image of deaf people and the usefulness and beauty of sign language.

In larger cities, and some smaller communities, there are clubs for the deaf. The organizations serve social and recreational purposes. They often sponsor athletic teams which compete in leagues with hearing teams. There are dances and cultural functions. As these clubs vary greatly in quality, it is wise for parents to visit and inquire about a given club before having their child attend.

Many ministers, rabbis, and priests provide time in their churches and temples for deaf worshipers. Services are conducted in speech and sign language. There are ordained deaf ministers in many denominations; and in others, hearing persons are given a special program to qualify them to serve the deaf. Some of the major religious organizations have auxiliaries specifically for the deaf.

The Council of Organizations Serving the Deaf** is a federation of major organizations of the deaf. It provides information about deafness for parents, professionals, and the general public, and helps its member organizations and the deaf community in relation to national and local issues. Its Annual Forum is a well-attended meeting.

The Gallaudet College Alumni Association (of the National College for the Deaf) is a worldwide organization. Gallaudet College, until 1968, was the world's only college exclusively for the deaf. Then, the National

---

* The central office address of the National Fraternal Association of the Deaf is 6701 West North Avenue, Oak Park, Illinois, 60302.

**Home office is 4201 Connecticut Avenue, N.W., Washington, D.C., 20008.

Technical Institute for the Deaf was established in Rochester, New York in 1968 as part of the Rochester Institute of Technology which serves a nondeaf population.

There is an Oral Deaf Adult Section of the Alexander Graham Bell Association for the Deaf. It has about 250 members. This group promotes the teaching of speech and speech reading.

The fallacious claim that oralism will enable the deaf person to better integrate with the nondeaf is demonstrated by the need for clubs exclusively for so-called oral deaf adults. At meetings, deaf members try to "talk" to and speech read other deaf persons. The existence of these clubs is testimony to the inability of most of these people to interact effectively and gratifyingly with the normally hearing.

Organizations and programs, large and small, national and local, exclusively for deaf people, play a truly important role in the lives of all deaf persons. Their leaders and members know best the implication of deafness. Yet, hearing rehabilitationists who have much influence on deaf education and on the subsequent status of deaf persons in society almost never consult the deaf. They have isolated themselves from the social contacts required to grasp fully the ramifications of deafness.

An analogous situation once existed among the blind. Blind leader fought for over a hundred years for the use of braille. Sighted people opposed the idea, ignoring the wishes of the blind. "The blind must read raised printed (standard alphabet) letters," they said emphatically. Finally Louis Braille, who was blind, found influential people who would listen, and the system of braille gained ascendacy. The blind, enabled to read, were educationally freed. The time has yet to come when the hearing man's deafness to the deaf man's needs is cured.

Not all organizations for deaf adults are constructive. Throughout the United States, there are semiorganized, quasi-criminal groups promoting what is called "peddling" but is actually begging. A deaf person approaches groups of hearing persons in bars, restaurants, or other public places with a trinket or cards showing the manual alphabet. To these trinkets or cards a message is attached: "I am deaf and cannot work. Please buy this." These people belong to organized groups or gangs, many of whom travel all over the country. The leaders are generally intelligent but unscrupulous deaf persons who control and exploit weaker or retarded deaf youths. On occasion, hearing persons have been apprehended masquerading as deaf in order to do this peddling. Sometimes individual sociopathic deaf peddlers will operate independently.

Peddlers may gross up to $600 per week. The deaf community holds these beggars in contempt, for they create a bad impression of other deaf people. The National Association for the Deaf has attempted to promote legislation against such peddling. Professionals, parents, and others render a service when they discourage or report these deaf beggars to the authorities. Such illicit activities would probably lose support if education and rehabilitation were more successful in better preparing deaf people for employment.

Mental Illness

Since the major consequence of deafness is social isolation, research projects have been conducted to determine the influence of this isolation on emotional development by examining the nature and the degree of mental illness in deaf people. A three-year research project to study the relationship of deafness to mental illness was conducted at the Psychosomatic and Psychiatric Institute of Michael Reese Hospital, Chicago, Illinois.[13] Some of the relevant findings are reported in the following.

The social isolation of deaf patients was far greater than that seen in other groups of mentally ill persons. Many of these patients were not only unable to exchange information on rudimentary needs with their families, but also had no close friends, deaf or hearing. Educated in the oral-only tradition and failing in that, many of them faced extreme frustration in their efforts to establish meaningful relationships.

The patients with better language and less severe illness responded better to therapy. However, a sizable number remained isolated. After years without real human contact, these patients were terrified by the efforts of others to establish closeness. Their lack of basic trust in other human beings made therapy difficult, if not impossible.

The extent to which deafness and its implications were denied by many families of these patients was eye-opening. The invisible nature of this denial allowed professionals in education, audiology, medicine, and related fields to encourage the parents to deny the real implications of deafness for the child's future (see chapter 2). Denial of irreversible deafness, a pathological yet common method of coping with the deaf child, prevents the development of constructive solutions. Its net effect is to leave the child and his family directing their energies inappropriately toward activities which are digressions from the realities of the situation. These digressions create fictitious versions of the deaf child.

One of the most disturbing findings of the Reese study was the pervasive underachievement of the outpatient population. This was particularly true of the seventeen percent diagnosed as "School Situation Reaction." These were deaf children without overt emotional difficulties who voluntarily came with their parents to the outpatient clinic for educational consultation. Many were teen-agers with average and above average intelligence whose level of education achievement was second or third grade. In fact, the median educational achievement of the clinic population was fourth-grade level. This and the impoverishment in general knowledge of social codes born of the limitations in communication resulted in an incapacitating naivete.

The failure of the educational system undermined efforts at psychotherapy and rehabilitation. The resulting inadequate educational foundation lessened the possibility of a hopeful prognosis. In addition, a lack of adequate parent-child comminication, deficient interaction with peers, and undereducation created therapeutic needs geared to bringing patients back to previous levels of functioning.

A common lack of sexual information was found to exist in the pa-

tient population studied at Michael Reese Hospital and among the deaf
population of New York State as studied by John Rainier and Kenneth
Altshuler.[14] This is a serious problem, for it affects the kinds of hetero-
sexual adaptations possible for deaf adults.

There is some disagreement regarding the relationship of deafness to
depressive illness. Earlier work by Altshuler suggested that pathological
depression was less prevalent among deaf adults due, in part, to their tendency to seek explanations in the environment for their internal difficulties.[15] An example of this is a situation in which a deaf person is refused a
job and assumes it is because the employer does not like deaf people. In
contrast, the individual in the typical depressed state, looks inward for explanations and develops guilt over the supposed "bad" motivations that he
discovers. That is, he blames himself for his failures. Both positions are
extremes. The normal individual strikes a successful compromise between
the two. He can objectively evaluate his environment and knows his personal limitations.

About six percent of the population seen at Michael Reese Hospital
had depressive illness as a primary diagnosis. Depressive affect was prominent in many other patients. Three of thirty-eight patients had made at
least one suicide attempt. Among the 121 outpatients, four had attempted
to take their own lives. The number who discussed suicide as "a way out"
was twice the number who tried it.

Ideally, in treatment, a deaf person should be helped to go beyond
his denial of deafness—to mourn the loss of the fantasy that hearing would
be regained, just as his parents earlier should have mourned the loss of
their wish for a perfect-hearing child. This period of mourning can be
followed by a realistic acceptance of the enduring implications of deafness,
which is a more comfortable psychological adaptation to deafness. Because a period of grief must come first, many people remain unconvinced
that giving up the denial is worth the effort. (For a more detailed discussion,
see the article, "Office Treatment of Private Deaf Patients," by Dr. David
Rothstein.*)

We found, in contrast to Rainer and Altshuler, that the frustrations
and loneliness born of the isolation lead to considerable depression in
deaf persons, especially those whose intellect and ambition are thwarted by
inappropriate educational and habilitative techniques and by the limitations of deafness. This reality and the isolation force the internalization of
thoughts of failure. This can intensify the depressive state.

John Rainer, et al, published their extensive study of psychotic illness
among deaf persons in 1963.[16] In it, types of psychotic illness present
among the deaf patients in state hospitals were compared to those found
among groups of hearing patients. It was found that schizophrenia, which
accounted for more than half of all hospitalized psychotic patients, was
not more common among the deaf patients admitted to the hospital than
among the hearing patients. However, deaf patients tended to stay in

---

*This is a chapter in the Grinker 1969 reference

state hospitals longer. Their deafness rendered them custodial patients because, until New York State established a unit for the deaf, there was generally no one available to communicate with them to initiate the rehabilitation process and no team to follow it up. The work of this unit and the work of others such as Luther Robinson at St. Elizabeth's Hospital in Washington, D.C., have demonstrated the tremendous advantage in grouping patients into a professionally staffed unit. These groups must have deep roots in the community to provide appropriate jobs, housing, and follow-up care after discharge.

An atypical finding among the New York deaf psychotic population was that five percent of those in state hospitals were found to have Usher's Syndrome, a genetic condition involving deafness and retinitis pigmentosa (progressive blindness.).[17] Sometimes mental deficiency is present as an additional feature of the disease.

Brain damage is believed to play a significant role in a number of the behavioral disorders of deaf persons. John Rainer and others have noted its role. McCay Vernon, in a series of articles on the total effects of the conditions* causing deafness, demonstrated that brain damage is intimately involved in an appreciable number of psychotic and lesser mental disorders.[18]

Past Vocational Adjustment And Future Trends

The demands of today's technological society limit vocational success for people saddled by deafness and their consequent undereducation. Even for the ambitious deaf student, self-education is difficult if not impossible when reading levels are third and fourth grade. The deaf have the same intelligence as the hearing. Despite this, they are frequently forced to do manual labor rather than appropriate professional or technical work. For example, eighty-seven percent of deaf people are employed in manual labor, as contrasted to less than fifty percent of the general population. Only seventeen percent of deaf people are white-collar workers compared to forty-six percent of the general population (see table 5). But what about the future?

Basic to future planning is a clear picture of current vocational trends and an understanding of their implications for deaf people. Unless realistic planning occurs now and needed changes in education and training are wrought within ten years, unemployment among deaf workers will be about seventy percent. Most of the remaining thirty percent of workers will be "dead-ended" in various unskilled and menial jobs. This is the prediction made by John A. Sessions, a labor authority for the AFL-CIO.[19]

What are the major trends now and in the predictable future that would have such a catastrophic effect for the deaf worker? There are five to be considered.

1. *There has been a shift from manual, semiskilled, and unskilled jobs to many more white-collar jobs.*[20] Manufacturing, where over half

---

*Meningitis, maternal rubella, blood-type incompatibility, premature birth, and genetic syndromes.

Table 5

Comparison of the Vocational Status of Deaf and Hearing Persons*

Vocational Status	Deaf	Hearing
Manual Labor	About 87 percent	Less than half
Manufacturing	Over half, most in manual labor	About one fourth of whom 25 percent are at management level
White Collar (Professional-Technical)	17 percent Crammate states this to be an over estimate	Over half
Urban Workers	Unknown	70 percent
Unemployed		
1. Washington, D. C.		
White men	4.3 percent	3.1 percent
White women	7.4 percent	1.9 percent
Negro men	16.9 percent	5.6 percent
Negro women	41.2 percent	5.7 percent
2. Southwest U. S. Young deaf adults	25 percent	11.2 percent
3. New England Young deaf adults	17 percent	11.2 percent
Civil Service	Exact data not available, but percent is small	15 percent

*This table reprinted from *Rehabilitation Literature* (in press). 1970.

of the deaf workers are employed, is an area of decreasing opportunity. Not only is the number of jobs in manufacturing not expected to keep pace, but the proportion of white-collar workers in manufacturing actually increased from sixteen percent in 1947, to twenty-five percent in 1966. And there is strong evidence that indicates an even greater shift in this direction. The deaf do the manual work of production; they are not white-collar employees in accounting, engineering, teaching, and technology. Traditionally, in these occupations there have been almost no deaf people.

2. *Of the 22,000 types of jobs listed in 1965,*[21] *over 6,000 were new since 1959 and over 8,000 that existed then are now extinct.* What are the implications? First, it means that flexibility and the capacity to be retrained are primary requirements for vocational survival. Because of the communicative and educational problems consequent to profound and severe hearing loss, workers have great difficulty in retraining programs—hence, vocational inflexibility. Second, it is no longer reasonable to expect that the original job training given a deaf person when he is young will allow him to rely on these same skills to maintain vocational viability throughout his years of employment. Vocational and rehabilitation counselors must recognize the need for special programs to retrain older deaf workers, men who are likely to have families and financial responsibilities.

3. *Educational requirements for employment are rapidly increasing. The average worker today spends thirty-three percent more years in school than his predecessor, and this trend is increasing.*[22] The number of jobs open to the functionally illiterate (thirty percent of deaf school dropouts are functionally illiterate) is rapidly shrinking. There are more jobs requiring at least a high school education. Even the jobs the illiterate can do are not open to them because when industry hires, it wants flexibility in the worker to permit future on-the-job training. Among the blue-collar workers, the highly trained craftsmen are in demand.

4. *Employment in the service sector will experience the fastest growth.*[23] The number of jobs in states and local governments will increase by forty-eight percent. Education, health care, recreation, and repair services are some of the areas that will experience similar demands for new workers, and this trend will continue. One out of every two new jobs created in the past decade has been in service industries. For the deaf worker, this is not encouraging. Civil service examinations usually require language skill well beyond a large majority of the deaf. In miscellaneous service industries, between fifty-five and eighty-eight percent are white-collar jobs. In the service industries, ten percent of the jobs are managerial; deaf persons are almost totally excluded from these. An additional fifty-five percent of employees in the service sector hold professional, technical, or clerical jobs.

5. *Seventy percent of Americans now live in the cities and suburbs.*[24] Although urbanization imposes certain hardships upon deaf people, it does offer one major advantage. With centralization, it is feasible to provide them professional-level counseling by social workers specifically trained in the use of manual communication and general knowledge about the meaning of deafness in their work. In the past, deaf clients were so widely scattered that such specialization was not economically practical. Consequently, the deaf client often had an unqualified counselor.

Jerome D. Schein, Director of the New York University Center for Research and Training in Deafness, addressed the February, 1970, Chicago Meeting of the Council of Organizations Serving the Deaf on "Social Services and the Deaf Client." In his address, he reported on his study of the extent to which deaf persons make use of available social agencies in Washington, D.C. Of 176 agencies surveyed, only 73 had rendered direct service to deaf clients. Of those 73, less than half had served more than one deaf person. There was at least one demand for every class of service: evaluation, therapy, recreation, welfare, family and child services, legal aid, et cetera. In a later study, deaf adults from the metropolitan Washington area were questioned about services they had requested from governmental agencies. [25] Nearly half had received some assistance from their state's division of vocational rehabilitation. Most striking was that only twelve of the seventy-three agencies which had served deaf persons made arrangements for manual communication. Only Gallaudet College and the Division of Vocational Rehabilitation of The State of Illinois had full-time professionals skilled in communicating with deaf persons.

These five major trends have created a vocational and educational crisis for the deaf population. How will they become self-supporting? The problem is not irresolvable. Deaf and hard of hearing people have the same intelligence as the normally hearing. Their work habits are good, and employers who have hired deaf workers, at times reluctantly, have generally been pleased.[26]

The answer lies in using an untapped potential for growth. It lies in providing proper and realistic educational opportunities through combined manual-oral communication, which breaks barriers to learning and to understanding and frees their normal intellectual capacity. To overcome the prognosis these trends suggest, counseling must be given which aids the deaf client in matching his unique combination of assets, liabilities, and interests with appropriate vocational positions. It must also prepare him to meet projected demands for skilled workers.

Notes
Chapter One

1. M. Vernon and B. Makowsky, "Deafness and Minority Group Dynamics," *Deaf American* 21 (1969): 3-6.
2. M. Vernon and E. D. Mindel, "Psychological and Psychiatric Aspects of Deafness," in *Audiological Assessment,* ed. D. Rose (New Jersey: Prentice-Hall, 1971) pp. 87-132.
3. *Ibid.*
4. *Ibid.*
5. June B. Miller, "Oralism," *Volta Review* 72 (1970): 211-17.
6. Vernon and Mindel, "Aspects of Deafness"; Miller, "Oralism," p. 211.
7. *Ibid.*
8. *Volta Review,* vols. 1-72.
9. Vernon and Mindel, "Aspects of Deafness."

Chapter Two

1. E. H. Lenneberg, *Biological Foundations of Language* (New York: John Wiley and Sons, Inc., 1967), pp. 158-78.
2. *Ibid.*
3. K. Z. Altshuler, "Personality Traits and Depressive Symptoms in the Deaf," in *Recent Advances in Biological Psychiatry,* ed. J. Wortis (New York: Plenum Press, 1963) 6: 63-72.
4. Angela Hefferman, "A Psychiatric Study of Fifty Children Referred to Hospital for Suspected Deafness," in *Emotional Problems of Childhood,* ed. Gerald Caplan (New York: Basic Books, 1955), pp. 269-92.
5. L. S. Cholden, *A Psychiatrist Works With Blindness* (New York: American Foundation for the Blind, 1958); D. A. Hamburg, "Psychological Adaptive Processes in Life Threatening Injuries" (Paper delivered at the Symposium on Stress, Walter Reed Medical Center, Washington, D.C., March 18, 1953).
6. M. Vernon, "Sociological and Psychological Factors Associated with Profound Hearing Loss," *Journal of Speech and Hearing Research* 12 (1969): 541-63.
7. E. D. Mindel, "A Child Psychiatrist Looks at Deafness," *Deaf American* 20 (February, 1968): 15-19.
8. *Ibid.*
9. R. G. Grinker, ed., "Psychiatric Diagnosis, Therapy, and Research on the Psychotic Deaf," Final Report Grant # RD-2407-S, Social Rehabilitation Service, Department of Health, Education, and Welfare, 1969 (Available from Dr. Grinker, Michael Reese Hospital, 2959 S. Ellis, Chicago, Illinois).

Chapter Three

1. M. Vernon, *Multiply Handicapped Deaf Children: Medical, Educational, and Psychological Aspects* (Washington, D.C.: Council of Exceptional Children, 1969); M. Vernon, "Multiply Handicapped Deaf Children: The Causes, Manifestations, and Significances of the Problem," *E.E.N.T. Digest* 31 (February, 1969): 40-58.
2. C. S. Karmody, "Asymptomatic Maternal Rubella and Congenital Deafness," *Archives of Otolaryngology* 89 (1969): 62-68; M. Vernon, "Rubella: An Introduction," *National Hearing Aid Journal* 22 (1968):4-22.
3. G. R. Fraser, "Profound Childhood Deafness," *Journal of Medical Genetics* 1 (1964):118-51; M. Vernon, "Current Etiological Factors in Deafness," *American Annals of the Deaf* 113 (1968):106-15.
4. H. Zellweger, "Genetics in Counseling," *Modern Medicine* 35 (1967): 40-51.
5. Vernon, *Handicapped Deaf Children: Aspects.*
6. *Ibid.*
7. Vernon, "Etiological Factors in Deafness," p. 1; M. Vernon, "Usher's Syndrome—Deafness and Progressive Blindness: Clinical Cases, Prevention, Theory, and Literature Survey," *Journal of Chronic Diseases* 22(1969):133-51.

8. Janet B. Hardy, G. R. G. Monif, and J. L. Sever, "Studies in Congenital Rubella, Baltimore 1964-1965. II. Clinic and Virologic," *Bulletin of the Johns Hopkins Hospital* 118 (1966):97-108; M. Vernon, "Characteristics Associated with Post Rubella Deaf Children," *Volta Review* 69 (1967):176-85.

9. Vernon, "Rubella: An Introduction," p. 4; D. E. Hicks, "Comparison of Profiles of Rubella and Non-rubella Deaf Children," *American Annals of the Deaf* 115 (1970):86-92.

10. Karmody, "Asymptomatic Maternal Rubella," p. 62.

11. Vernon, "Rubella: An Introduction," p. 4; Hicks, "Comparison of Profiles," p. 86.

12. Hardy, Monif, and Sever, "Studies in Rubella," p. 97.

13. Vernon, *Handicapped Deaf Children: Aspects;* Karmody, "Asymptomatic Maternal Rubella," p. 62; Hardy, Monif, and Sever, "Studies in Rubella," p. 97.

14. Karmody, "Asymptomatic Maternal Rubella," p. 62; Hardy, Monif, and Sever, "Studies in Rubella," p. 97.

15. E. B. Buynak et al., "Combined Live Measles and Rubella Virus Vaccines," *Journal of the American Medical Association* 207 (1969):2259-62.

16. Hardy, Monif, and Sever, "Studies in Rubella," p. 97.

17. Vernon, *Handicapped Deaf Children: Aspects;* M. Vernon, "Prematurity and Deafness: The Magnitude and Nature of the Problem Among Deaf Children," *Exceptional Children*, 38 (1967): 289-98; M. Vernon, "RH Factor and Deafness: The Problem, Its Psychological, Physical and Educational Manifestations," *Exceptional Children* 38 (1967): 5-12.

18. P. S. Paine, "Kernicterus," *Clinical Proceedings* 24 (1968):37-47.

19. M. Vernon, "Clinical Phenomena of Cerebral Palsy and Deafness," *Exceptional Children* 36 (1970): 743-51.

20. Paine, "Kernicterus," p. 37.

21. Vernon, "Prematurity and Deafness," p. 289.

22. *Ibid.*

23. Paine, "Kernicterus," p. 37.

24. Vernon, "RH Factor and Deafness," p. 5; Paine, "Kernicterus," p. 37; Vernon, "Clinical Phenomena." p. 743.

25. Vernon, "RH Factor and Deafness," p. 5; Vernon, "Clinical Phenomena." p. 743.

26. C. A. Clarke, "The Prevention of 'Rhesus' Babies," *Scientific American* 219 (1968):46-52.

27. *Ibid.*

28. M. Vernon, "Meningitis and Deafness," *Laryngoscope* 77 (1967): 1856-74; M. N. Swartz and P. R. Dodge," Bacterial Meningitis—A Review of Selected Aspects. II. Special Neurologic Problems, Postmeningitic Complications and Clinopathical Correlations," *New England Journal of Medicine* 272 (1965):954-62.

29. Vernon, "Meningitis and Deafness," p. 1856; Swartz and Dodge, "Bacterial Meningitis—Special Neurological Problems," p. 954.

30. Vernon, "Meningitis and Deafness," p. 1856.

31. Swartz and Dodge, "Bacterial Meningitis—Special Neurological Problems," p. 954.

32. M. N. Swartz and P. R. Dodge, "Bacterial Meningitis—A Review of Selected Aspects. I. General Clinical Features, Special Problems, and Unusual Meningeal Reactions in Mimicking Bacterial Meningitis," *New England Journal of Medicine* 272 (1965): 725-30.

33. Vernon, "Meningitis and Deafness," p. 1856.

34. *Ibid*, Swartz and Dodge, "Bacterial Meningitis—General Clinical Features," p. 725.

35. *Ibid.*

Chapter Four

1. Hayes A. Newby, "Special Problems in Hearing Testing," in *Audiology: Principles and Practices,* 2nd ed. (New York: Appleton-Century-Crofts, 1964) pp. 185-201.

2. John O'Neil and Herbert Oyer, "Testing Hearing of Children," in *Applied Audiometry* (New York: Dodd, Mead and Co., 1952) pp. 253-268.

3. Ira J. Hirsh, *The Measurement of Hearing* (New York: McGraw-Hill Book Co., 1966).

4. Hallowell Davis and S. Richard Silverman, *Hearing and Deafness* (New York: Holt, Rinehart and Winston, 1970); D. E. Rose, ed., *Audiological Assessment* (New Jersey: Prentice-Hall, 1970-).

5. Davis and Silverman, *Hearing and Deafness.*

6. Rose, *Audiological Assessment.*

7. Davis and Silverman, *Hearing and Deafness.*

8. Herbert Oyer, "Auditory Perception," in *Auditory Communication for the Hard of Hearing* (New Jersey: Prentice-Hall, 1966) pp. 26-45.

9. Rose, *Audiological Assessment.*

10. Davis and Silverman, *Hearing and Deafness;* Rose, *Audiological Assessment.*

11. J. H. Macrae, "Deterioration of the Residual Hearing of Children with Sensorineural Deafness," *Acta Oto-Laryngologica* 66 (1968):33-39.

12. Marion Downes, "Early Primary Screening," *Acta Oto-Laryngologica Supplementum* (Proceedings of a conference on the young deaf child; Identification and management, Toronto, Canada, Oct 8-9, 1964) 206:39-44.

13. B. E. Hoffmeyer, "Schools Society Asked to Adjust," *California News* 85 (1970):3-6.

14. D. E. Rose and W. M. Shearer, "Cortical Audiometry for Children," *E.E.N.T. Digest* 30 (1968): 61-64.

15. Rose, *Audiological Assessment.*

16. Hoffmeyer, "Schools Asked to Adjust," p. 3.

17. Rose, *Audiological Assessment.*

18. Mindel, "A Child Psychiatrist Looks at Deafness," p. 15.

19. Helmer Myklebust, *Auditory Disorders in Children* (New York: Gruen & Stratton, 1954).

20. Mindel, "A Child Psychiatrist Looks at Deafness," p. 15.

21. R. F. Nagel, "Audiology and the Education of the Deaf," *Journal of Speech and Hearing Disorders,* 27 (1962):188-90.

Chapter Five

1. René A. Spitz, *The First Year of Life* (New York: International Universities Press, Inc., 1965); Anna Freud, "The Concept of Developmental Lines," in *The Psychoanalytic Study of the Child* (New York: International Universities Press, Inc., 1963)18:245-65; E. H. Erikson, *Childhood and Society* (New York: W. W. Norton, 1950); H. S. Sullivan, *Interpersonal Theory of Psychiatry* (New York: W. W. Norton, 1953); P. Mullany, *Contributions of Harry Stack Sullivan* (New York: Hermitage Press, 1952).

2. Eric H. Lenneberg, *Biological Foundations;* Eric H. Lenneberg, "What Is Meant By a Biological Approach to Language," *American Annals of the Deaf* 115 (1970):67-72; Eric H. Lenneberg, "On Explaining Language," *Science* 164 (1969): 635-43.

3. Lenneberg, *Biological Foundations.*

4. *Ibid.*

5. P. Polak, R. Emde, and R. A. Spitz, "The Smiling Response. II. Visual Discrimination and the Onset of Depth Perception," *Journal on Nervous and Mental Diseases* 139 (1964):407-15.

6. Lenneberg, *Biological Foundations.*

7. *Ibid.*

8. *Ibid.*

9. Freda G. Rebelsky, Raymond H. Starr, Jr., and Zella Luria, "Language Development the First Four Years," in *Infancy and Early Childhood,* ed., Yvonne Brackbill (New York: The Free Press 1967(pp. 289-300).

10. Lenneberg, *Biological Foundations.*

11. *Ibid.*

12. Patricia Greenfield, "Development of the Holophrase," Harvard University, Center for Cognitive Studies, 1968).

13. *Ibid.*

14. Grinker, "Psychiatric Diagnosis."

15. Lenneberg, *Biological Approach to Language,* p. 67; Edna Simon Levine, *The Psychology of Deafness* (New York: Columbia University Press, 1960) pp. 27-55; H. Myklebust, *The Psychology of Deafness* (New York: Grune & Stratton, 1960); Altshuler, "Traits and Symptoms in the Deaf," p. 63.

16. W. N. Craig and J. L. Collins, "Analysis of Communicative Interaction in Classes for Deaf Children," *American Annals of the Deaf* 115 (1970):79-85.

17. Mary E. Switzer and B. R. Williams, "Life Problems of Deaf People," *Archives of Environmental Health* 15 (1967):249-56; B. R. Williams and M. Vernon, "Vocational Guidance," in *Hearing and Deafness,* 3rd ed. rev., eds., H. Davis and S. R. Silverman (New York: Holt, Rinehart, and Winston, 1970).

18. Lenneberg, *Biological Foundations.*

19. *Ibid.*

20. *Ibid.*
21. *Ibid.*
22. *Ibid.;* David McNeill, "The Capacity for Language Acquisition" (Paper delivered at Conference of Research on Behavioral Aspects of Deafness, New Orleans, La., May, 1965 Available from U. S. Department of Health, Education and Welfare, Washington, D.C. pp. 11-28; David McNeil, "Developmental Psycholinguistics in *The Genesis of Language: A Psycholinguistic Approach,* eds., Frank Smith and George A. Miller (Cambridge, Mass.: M.I.T. Press), pp. 15-84; Donald Moores, "Communication, Psycholinguistics, and Deafness" (Proceedings of the Teachers Institute, Maryland School for the Deaf, Oct. 17, 1969) pp. 4-15. David McNeill, "The Creation of Language," *Discovery* 27 (1966):34-38.
23. *Ibid.*
24. *Ibid.*
25. Lenneberg, *Biological Foundations;* McNeill, "Language Acquisitions."
26. Noam Chomsky, "The General Property of Language," in *Brain Mechanisms Underlying Speech and Language,* ed. F. L. Dailey (Proceedings of a conference held at Princeton, N.Y., Nov. 9-12, 1965) pp. 73-88.
27. Edna A. Adler, "Reading Out Loud in the Language of Signs," *American Annals of the Deaf,* 109 (1964):364-66.
28. Hardy, Monif, and Sever, "Studies in Rubella," p. 97; Vernon, *Handicapped Deaf Children: Aspects;* Vernon, "Characteristics Associated with Post Rubella," p. 176.
29. D. E. Hicks, "Comparison of Profiles," p. 86.
30. D. W. Brown, "A Contemporary Psycho-educational Approach to Mental Health and Deafness," in *The Mentally Retarded Deaf Child,* eds., H. W. Bralje and B. R. Wolff (A summary report of 1969 Summer Institute on the Multiply Handicapped, Lewis and Clark College, Portland, Oregon), p. 71-78.
31. M. Vernon, "Fifty Years of Research on the Intelligence of Deaf and Hard of Hearing Children: A Review of Literature and Discussion of Implications," *Journal on Rehabilitation of the Deaf* 1 (1968):4-7.
32. Vernon, *Handicapped Deaf Children: Aspects.*
33. Lenneberg, *Biological Foundations.*

Chapter Six

1. W. C. Stokoe, "Sign Language Structure: An outline of the Visual Communication Systems of the American Deaf," Studies in Linguistics (Buffalo, N.Y.: University of Buffalo Press, 1960).
2. Vernon, "Profound Hearing Loss," p. 541.
3. Lenneberg, "Biological Approach to Language," p. 67.
4. Vernon, "Profound Hearing Loss," p. 541.
5. Mindel, "A Child Psychiatrist Looks at Deafness," p. 15; M. Vernon, "Mental Health, Deafness and Communication" (Frederick County: Maryland School for Deaf; Washington, D.C.: Council of Organizations Serving the Deaf, 1969), pp. 16-21.
6. P. Ekman and W. V. Freisen, "Nonverbal Behavior in Psychotherapy Research," in *Research in Psychotherapy* (Washington, D.C.: American Psychological Association, 1968), pp. 179-216.
7. H. R. Kohl, "Language and Education of the Deaf" (A Publication of The Center for Urban Education, 33 W. 42nd Street, New York) 1966; J. Ridgeway, "Dumb Children," *New Republic* 161 (1969):19-21.
8. Stokoe, "Sign Language Structure."
9. A. V. Cicourel and R. J. Boese, "Sign Language Acquisition and the Teaching of Deaf Children," in *The Functions of Language: An Anthropological and Psychological Approach,* eds., D. Hymes, C. Cazden, and V. John (New York: Teachers College Press, 1970-).
10. Kathryn P. Meadow, "Early Manual Communication in Relation to the Deaf Child's Intellectual, Social, and Communicative Functioning," *American Annals of the Deaf* 113 (1968):29-41; M. Vernon and S. D. Koh, "Effects of Early Manual Communication on Achievement of Deaf Children," *American Annals of the Deaf* (1970-); Vol. 115, pp. 527-536; E. R. Stuckless and J. W. Birch, "The Influence of Early Manual Communication on the Linguistic Development of Deaf Children," *American Annals of the Deaf III* (1966):452-62; G. W. Montgomery, "Relationship of Oral Skills to Manual Communication in Profoundly Deaf Students," *American Annals of the Deaf III* (1966): 557-65; E. A. Sevenson, "A Study of the Educational Achievement of Deaf Children of Deaf Parents" (Berkeley: California School for the Deaf,

1964); S. P. Quigley and D. Frisina, *Institutionalized and Psychoeducational Development in Deaf Children*, Council for Exceptional Children Research Monograph, Series A, no. 3, 1961; M. S. Hestor, "Manual Communication" ed. P. V. Doctor (Report of the Proceedings of the Interior Congress on Educating of Deaf and the 41st meeting of American Instructors of the Deaf, Gallaudet College, Washington, D.C., 1963) pp. 211-221; S. P. Quigley, "The Influence of Finger Spelling on the Development of Language, Communication, and Education Achievement of Children" (Proceedings of the 42nd Meeting of the Convention of American Instructors of the Deaf, Flint, Michigan, 1964), pp. 428-38.

11. Mindel, "A Child Psychiatrist Looks at Deafness," p. 15.
12. Meadow, "Manual Communication," p. 29.
13. Stevenson, "Study of the Educational Achievement in Deaf Children."
14. Quigley and Frisina, Institutionalization; Quigley, "Influence of Finger Spelling."
15. *Ibid.*
16. Quigley and Frisina, *Institutionalization.*
17. Montgomery, "Relationships of Oral Skills," p. 557.
18. Vernon, "Profound Hearing Loss," p. 541.
19. Grinker, "Psychiatric Diagnosis."
20. E. L. Scouten, "The Prelingual Deaf Child and His Oral Education in a New Perspective," *American Annals of the Deaf* 114 (1969): 770-76.

Chapter Seven

1. H. G. Furth, *Thinking Without Language* (New York: The Free Press, 1966).
2. M. Vernon, "The Relationship of Language to the Thinking Process," *Archives of General Psychiatry* 16 (1967):325-33; Vernon and Mindel, "Aspects of Deafness."
3. E. B. Boatner, "The Need of a Realistic Approach to the Education of the Deaf" (Paper delivered to the joint convention of the California Association of Parents of Deaf and Hard of Hearing Children, California Association of Teachers of the Deaf and Hard of Hearing, and the California Association of the Deaf, November 6, 1965); W. J. McClure, "Current Problems and Trends in the Education of the Deaf," *Deaf American* 18 (1966):8-14; J. W. Wrightstone, M. S. Aronow and Sue Muskowitz, "Developing Reading Test Norms for Deaf Children," *American Annals of the Deaf* 108 (1963):311-316; J. D. Schein and S. Bushnaq, "Higher Education for the Deaf in the United States—A Retrospective Investigation," *American Annals of the Deaf* 107 (1962):416-420; H. D. Babbidge, "Education of the Deaf" (a Report to the Secretary of Health, Education & Welfare by his Advisory Committee on the Education of the Deaf, [Available from Dept. of H.E.W.]).
4. Kohl, "Language and Education of the Deaf,"; D. F. Moores, "An Investigation of the Psycholinguistic Functioning of Deaf Adolescents," *Exceptional Children* 36 (1970): 645-652.
5. W. N. Craig, "Effects of Preschool Training on the Development of Reading and Lipreading Skills of Deaf Children," *American Annals of the Deaf* 109 (1964):280-296; W. D. Phillips, "Influence of Preschool Training on Achievement in Language Arts, Arithmetic Concepts, and Socialization of Young Deaf Children" (Doctoral diss., Teachers College, Columbia, 1963).
6. Vernon, "Etiological Factors in Deafness,",p. 106.
7. E. L. Lowell, "Research in Speechreading: Some Relationships to Language Development and Implications for the Classroom Teacher" (Report of the proceedings of the 39th Meeting of the Convention of American Instructors of the Deaf, 1959), pp. 68-73.
8. *Ibid.*
9. Vernon, "Etiological Factors in Deafness," p. 106.
10. J. D. Rainer et al., eds., *Family and Mental Health Problems in a Deaf Population* (New York: New York State Psychiatric Institute, 1963).
11. *Ibid.*
12. Vernon and Makowsky, "Deafness and Minority Dynamics," p. 3.
13. Grinker, "Psychiatric Diagnosis."
14. Rainer, *Problems in a Deaf Population.*
15. Altshuler, "Traits and Symptoms in the Deaf," p. 63.
16. Rainer, *Problems in a Deaf Population.*
17. Vernon, "Usher's Syndrome," p. 133.
18. Vernon, *Handicapped Deaf Children: Aspects.*

19. J. A. Sessions, "Automation and the Deaf" (A paper presented to the Leadership Training Program in Deafness, San Fernando Valley State College, June 18, 1966).
20. M. Friedman, "The Changing Profile of the Labor Force," *AFL-CIO American Federalist* 74 (1967): 7-14.
21. *Ibid.*
22. *Ibid.*
23. Vernon, "Profound Hearing Loss," p. 541.
24. Friedman, "Changing Profile," p. 7.
25. J. D. Schein, *The Deaf Community* (Washington, D.C.; Gallaudet Press, 1968).
26. P. H. Furfey and T. J. Harte, *Instruction of Deaf and Hearing in Frederick County* (Washington, D.C.: Catholic University Press, 1964).

References Cited

Adler, Edna A. 1964. Reading out loud in the language of signs. *American Annals of the Deaf.* 109:364-366.

Altschuler, K. Z. 1963. Personality traits and depressive symptoms in the deaf. *In Recent Advances in Biological Psychiatry,* ed. J. Wortis, 6:63-72. New York: Plenum Press.

Babbidge, H. D. Education of the deaf. A report to the Secretary of Health, Education and Welfare by the Advisory Committee on the Education of the Deaf. Dept. of H.E.W.

Boatner, E. B. 1965. The need of a realistic approach to the education of the deaf. A Paper delivered to the joint convention of the California Association of Parents of Deaf and Hard of Hearing Children, California Association of Teachers of the Deaf and Hard of Hearing, and the California Association of the Deaf.

Brown, D. W. 1965. A contemporary psycho-educational approach to mental health and deafness. In *The Mentally Retarded Deaf Child,* eds., H. W. Bralje and B. R. Wolff, pp. 71-78. A summary report of the Summer Institute on the Multiply Handicapped, Lewis and Clark College, Portland, Oregon.

Buynak, E. B.; Weibol, R. E.; Whitman, J. E.; Stokes, J. and Hilleman, M. R. 1969. Combined live measles and rubella virus vaccines. *Journal of the American Medical Association.* 207: 2259-62.

Cholden, L. S. 1958. *A Psychiatrist Works With Blindness.* New York: American Foundation for the Blind.

Chomsky, Noam. 1965. The general property of language. In *Brain Mechanisms Underlying Speech and Language,* ed. F. L. Dailey, pp. 73-88. Proceedings of a conference held 9-12 Nov. 1965, in Princeton, New Jersey.

Cicourel, A. V., and Boese, R. J. 1970-. Sign language acquisition and the teaching of deaf children. In *The Functions of Language: An Anthropological and Psychological Approach,* eds., D. Hymes, C. Cazden, and V. John. New York: Teachers College Press.

Clarke, C. A. 1968 The prevention of "rhesus" babies. *Scientific American.* 219:46-52.

Craig, W. N. 1964. Effects of preschool training on the development of reading and lipreading skills of deaf children. *American Annals of the Deaf.* 199: 280-296.

Craig, W. N., and Collins, J. L. 1970. Analysis of communicative interaction in classes for deaf children. *American Annals of the Deaf.* 115:79-85.

Davis, Hallowell, and Silverman, S. Richard. 1970. Hearing and Deafness. New York: Holt, Rinehart and Winston.

Denton, D. M. 1964. Early primary screening. *Acta Oto-laryngologica Supplementum.* 206:39-44. Proceedings of a conference on The Young Deaf Child: Identification and Management, 8-9 Oct. 1964, in Toronto, Canada.

Downes, Marion. 1964. Early primary screening. *Acta Oto-Laryngologica Supplementum,* 206: 39-44. Proceedings of a Conference on the Young Deaf Child; Identification and Management, 8-9 Oct. 1964 in Toronto, Canada.

Ekman, P., and Freisen, W. V. 1968. Nonverbal behavior in Psychotherapy research. In *Research in Psychotherapy,* pp. 179-216. Washington, D.C.: American Psychological Association.

Erikson, E. H. 1950. *Childhood and Society.* New York: W. W. Norton.

Fraser, G. R. Profound childhood deafness. *Journal of Medical Genetics.* 1:118-51.

Freud, Anna. 1963. The concept of developmental lines. In *The Psychoanalytic Study of the Child.* 18:245-265. New York: International Universities Press.

Friedman, M. 1967. The Changing profile of the labor force, *AFL-CIO American Federalist.* 74: 7-14.

Furfey, P. H., and Harte, T. J. 1964. *Interaction of Deaf and Hearing in Frederick County.* Washington, D. C.: Catholic University.

Furth, H. G. 1966. *Thinking Without Language.* New York: Free Press.

Greenfield, Patricia. 1968. Development of the Holophrase. Harvard University. Center for Cognitive Studies.

Grinker, R. G., ed. 1969. Psychiatric diagnosis, therapy, and research of the psychotic deaf. Final Report Grant # RD-2407-S, Social Rehabilitation Service, Dept. of H.E.W. Available from Dr. Grinker, Michael Reese Hospital, 2959 S. Ellis, Chicago, Illinois.

Hamburg, D. A. 1953. Psychological adaptive processes in life threatening injuries. A Paper delivered at the Symposium on Stress, 18 March 1953, at Walter Reed Medical Center, Washington, D.C.

Hardy, Janet B., Monif, G. R. G., and Sever, J. L. 1966. Studies in congenital rubella, Baltimore 1964-1965, II clinic and virologic. *Bulletin of the Johns Hopkins Hospital.* 118: 97-108.

Hefferman, Angela. 1955. A psychiatric study of fifty children referred to hospital for suspected deafness. In *Emotional Problems of Childhood,* ed. Gerald Caplan, pp. 269-292. New York: Basic Books.

Hester, M. S. 1963. Manual communication. In a report of the proceedings of International Congress on Education of the Deaf and the 41st Meeting of American Instructors of the Deaf, pp. 211-221. Gallaudet College, Washington, D. C.

Hicks, D. E. 1970. Comparison of profiles of rubella and non-rubella deaf children. *American Annals of the Deaf.* 115:86-92.

Hirsh, Ira J. 1966. *The Measurement of Hearing.* New York: McGraw-Hill.

Hoffmeyer, B. E. 1970. *Schools society asked to adjust.* North Carolina School Paper 85:3-6.

Karmody, C. S. 1969. Asymptomatic maternal rubella and congenital deafness. *Archives of Otolaryngology.* 89:62-68.

Kohl, H. R. 1966. Language and education of the deaf. A publication of The Center for Urban Education, 33 W. 42nd Street, New York.

Lenneberg, E. H. 1967. *Biological Foundations of Language.* New York: John Wiley and Sons, Inc.

– – –. 1969. On explaining language. *Science.* 164: 635-43.

– – –. 1970. What is meant by a biological approach to language? *American Annals of the Deaf.* 115: 67-72.

Levine, Edna Simon. 1960. *The Psychology of Deafness.* pp. 27-55. New York: Columbia University Press.

Lowell, E. L. 1959. Research in Speechreading: some relationships to language development and implications for the classroom teacher. A report of the proceedings of the 39th Meeting of the Convention of American Instructors of the Deaf. pp. 68-73.

McClure, W. J. 1966. Current problems and trends in the education of the deaf. *Deaf American.* 18:8-14.

Macrae, J. H. 1968. Deterioration of the residual hearing of children with sensorineural deafness. *Acta Oto-laryngological.* 66:33-39.

McNeill, David. 1965. The capacity for language acquisition. A paper delivered at the Conference of Research on Behavioral Aspects of Deafness, May 1965, in New Orleans, La. pp. 11-28. Available from Dept. of H.E.W., Washington, D.C.

– – –. 1966. Developmental Psycholinguistics. In *The Genesis of Language: a psycholinguistic approach,* ed. Frank Smith and George A. Miller. Cambridge, Mass.: MIT Press.

– – –. 1966. The creation of language. *Discovery.* 27:34-38.

Meadow, Kathryn. 1968. Early manual communication in relation to the deaf child's intellectual, social, and communicative functioning. *American Annals of the Deaf.* 113:29-41.

Miller, June B. 1970. Oralism. *Volta Review.* 72:211-17.

Mindel, E. D. 1968. A child psychiatrist looks at deafness. *Deaf American.* 20:15-19.

Moores, Donald. 1969. Communication, psycholinguistics, and deafness. Proceedings of The Teachers Institute, 17 Oct. 1969, at Maryland School for the Deaf.

– – –. 1970. An investigation of the psycholinguistic functioning of deaf adolescents. *Exceptional Children.* 36:645-52.

Montgomery, G. W. 1966. Relationship of roal skills to manual communication in profoundly deaf students. *American Annals of the Deaf.* 3:557-65.

Mullahy, P. 1952. *Contributions of Harry Stack Sullivan.* New York: Hermitage Press.

Myklebust, Helmer. 1954. *Auditory Disorders in Children.* New York: Gruen & Stratton.

– – –. 1960. *The Psychology of Deafness.* New York: Grune & Stratton.

Nagel, R. F. 1962. Audiology and the education of the deaf. *Journal of Speech and Hearing Disorders.* 27:188-90.

Newby, Hayes A. 1964. Special problems in hearing testing. In *Audiology: Principles and Practices,* 2nd ed., pp. 185-201. New York: Appleton-Century-Crofts.

O'Neil, John, and Oyer, Herbert. 1952. Testing hearing of children. In *Applied Audiometry,* pp. 253-68. New York: Dodd, Mead and Co.

Oyer, Herbert. 1966. Auditory perception. In *Auditory Communication for the Hard of Hearing,* pp. 26-45. New Jersey: Prentice-Hall.

Paine, P. S. 1968. Kernicterus. *Clinical Proceedings.* 24:37-47.

Phillips, W. D. 1963. Influence of preschool training on achievement in language arts, arithmetic concepts, and socialization of young deaf children. Doctoral diss., Teachers College, Columbia.

Polak, P. R.; Emde, R.; and Spitz, R. A. 1964. The smiling response. II. Visual discrimination and the onset of depth perception. *Journal of Nervous and Mental Diseases.* 139:407-15.

Quigley, S. P. 1968. The influence of finger spelling on the development of language, communication, and educational achievement in deaf children. Mimeographed. University of Illinois, Department of Special Education.

Quigley, S. P., and Frisina, D. 1961. Institutionalized and psychoeducational development in deaf children. Council for Exceptional Children Research Monograph, Series A, no. 3.

Rainer, J. D.; Altshuler, K. Z.; Kollmann, F. J.; Demings, W. E., eds. 1963. *Family and Mental Health Problems in a Deaf Population.* New York: New York State Psychiatric Institute.

Rebelsky, Freda G.; Starr, Raymond H., Jr.; Luria, Zella. 1967. Language development the first four years. In *Infancy and Early Childhood,* ed. Yvonne Brackbill, pp. 289-300. New York: Free Press.

Ridgeway, J. 1969. Dumb children. *New Republic.* 161:19-21.

Rose, D. E., and Shearer, W. M. 1968. Cortical audiometry for children. *E.E.N.T. Digest.* 30:61-64.

Rose, D.E., ed. 1970-. *Audiological Assessment.* New Jersey: Prentice-Hall.

Schein, J. D. 1968. *The Deaf Community.* Washington, D.C.: Gallaudet Press.

Schein, J. D., and Bushnaq, S. 1962. Higher education for the deaf in the United States—a retrospective investigation. *American Annals of the Deaf.* 107: 416-20.

Scouten, E. L. 1969. The prelingual deaf child and his oral education in a new perspective. *American Annals of the Deaf.* 114:770-76.

Sessions, J. A. 1966. Automation and the Deaf. A paper delivered to the Leadership Training Program in Deafness, 8 June 1966, at San Fernando Valley State College.

Spitz, René A. 1965. The First Year of Life. New York: International Universities Press, Inc.

Stevenson, E. A. 1964. A study of the educational achievement of deaf children of deaf parents. Berkeley: California School for the Deaf.

Stokoe, W. C. 1960. Sign language structure: an outline of the visual communication systems of the American deaf. In *Studies in Linguistics.* Buffalo, New York: University of Buffalo Press.

Stuckless, E. R., and Birch, J. W. 1966. The influence of the early manual communication on the linguistic development of deaf children. *American Annals of the Deaf.* 3:452-62.

Sullivan, H. S. 1953. *Interpersonal Theory of Psychiatry.* New York: W. W. Norton.

Swartz, M. N., and Dodge, P. R. 1965. Bacterial meningitis—a review of selected aspects. I. General clinical features, special problems, and unusual meningeal reactions in mimicking bacterial meningitis. *New England Journal of Medicine* 272:725-30.

— — —. 1965. Bacterial meningitis—a review of selected aspects. II. special neurologic problems, postmeningitic complications and clinicopathological correlations. *New England Journal of Medicine.* 272:954-62.

Switzer, Mary E., and Williams, B. R. 1967. Life problems of deaf people. *Archives of Environmental Health.* 15:249-56.

Vernon, M. 1967. Characteristics associated with post-rubella deaf children. *Volta Review.* 69:176-85.

— — —. 1967. Meningitis and deafness. *Laryngoscope.* 77:1856-74.

— — —. 1967. Prematurity and deafness: the magnitude and nature of the problem among deaf children. *Exceptional Children.* 38:289-98.

— — —. 1967. The relationship of language to the thinking process. *Archives of General Psychiatry.* 16:325-33.

— — —. 1967. RH factor and deafness: the problem, its psychological, physical and educational manifestations. *Exceptional Children.* 38:5-12.

— — —. 1968. Current etiological factors in deafness. *American Annals of the Deaf.* 113:106-15.

— — —. 1968. Fifty years of research on the intelligence of deaf and hard of hearing children: a review of literature and discussion of implications. *Journal on Rehabilitation of the Deaf.* 1.4-7.

— — —. 1968. Rubella: an introduction. *National Hearing Aid Journal.* 22:4-22.

— — —. 1969. Multiply handicapped deaf children: the causes, manifestations, and significances of the problem. *E.E.N.T. Digest.* 31:40-58.

— — —. 1969. *Multiply Handicapped Deaf Children: Medical, Educational, and Psychological Aspects.* Washington D.C.: Council of Exceptional Children.

— — —. 1969. Mental Health, deafness, and communication. Frederick County: Maryland School for Deaf; Washington D.C.: Council of Organizations Serving the Deaf.

— — —. 1969. Sociological and psychological factors associated with profound hearing loss. *Journal of Speech and Hearing Research.* 12:541-63.

— — —. 1969. Usher's syndrome — deafness and progressive blindness: clinical cases, prevention, theory, and literature survey. *Journal of Chronic Diseases.* 22:133-51.

— — —. 1970-. Clinical phenomena of cerebral palsy and deafness. *Exceptional Children.* 36:743-751.

Vernon, M., and Koh, S. D. 1970 vol. 115: pp. 527-536. Effects of early manual communication on achievement of deaf children. *American Annals of the Deaf.*

Vernon, M., and Makowsky, B. 1969. Deafness and minority group dynamics. *Deaf American.* 21:3-6.

Vernon, M., and Mindel, E. D. 1971 pp. 87-132. Psychology and psychiatric aspects of deafness. In *Audiological Assessment,* ed. D. Rose, New Jersey: Prentice-Hall

Williams, B. R., and Vernon, M. 1970 pp. 457-479. Vocational guidance. In *Hearing and Deafness,* 3rd ed. rev., eds. H. Davis and S. R. Silverman, New York: Holt, Rinehart, and Winston.

Wrightstone, J. W.; Aronow, M. S.; and Muskowitz, Sue. 1963. Developing reading test norms for deaf children. *American Annals of the Deaf.* 108:311-16.

Zellweger, H. 1967. Genetics in counseling. *Modern Medicine.* 35:40-51.

INDEX